THE
FIRST AMERICAN
COOKBOOK

A FACSIMILE
of *"American Cookery,"* 1796

by

Amelia Simmons

With an Essay by
Mary Tolford Wilson

DOVER PUBLICATIONS, INC.
NEW YORK

Published in Canada by General Publishing Company, Ltd., 30 Lesmill Road, Don Mills, Toronto, Ontario.
Published in the United Kingdom by Constable and Company, Ltd.

This Dover edition, first published in 1984, is an unabridged and unaltered republication of *American Cookery*, as published by Oxford University Press, New York, in 1958. The present edition is published with the permission of Oxford University Press, and of *The William and Mary Quarterly: A Magazine of Early American History*, in which the Wilson essay originally appeared (3d Ser., Vol. XIV, No. 1, January 1957; copyright 1957 by the Institute of Early American History and Culture). The perfect copy of the original edition of *American Cookery* used for the 1958 Oxford edition was reproduced by courtesy of the American Antiquarian Society.

Manufactured in the United States of America
Dover Publications, Inc., 31 East 2nd Street, Mineola, N.Y. 11501

Library of Congress Cataloging in Publication Data

Simmons, Amelia.
　　The first American cookbook.

　　Reprint. Originally published: American cookery. New York: Oxford University Press, 1958.
　　1. Cookery, American — Early works to 1800. I. Simmons, Amelia. American cookery. II. Title.
TX703.S53　　1984　　　　641.5973　　　　84-4205
ISBN 0-486-24710-4

CONTENTS

———————

THE FIRST AMERICAN COOKBOOK

MARY TOLFORD WILSON

LONG after Stephen Day had begun the operation of a printing press in the infant Massachusetts Bay colony, the American who sought printed guidance in almost any branch of temporal affairs was still forced to rely upon European works. "Those that walk mournfully with God" might turn to Richard Standfast's *Little Handful of Cordial Comforts for Fainting Souls,*[1] printed in Boston, or to any of the numerous sermons that flowed from colonial American presses; but the man who needed to know the best time to plant his wheat and the housewife whose receipt for syllabub was not completely to her taste could find help only in imported books.

For aid in such mundane matters, the English-speaking colonist might bring with him Thomas Tusser's *Five Hundreth Pointes of Good Husbandrie,* first printed in 1573 and frequently reissued. This work was doubly desirable because it also contained a section devoted to *Huswiferie.*[2] The rhymed advice in Tusser's appealing book covered every aspect of life on the land and in the house, from sowing "peason and beans, in the wane of the moone," to marking new blankets and sheets. However, from the housewife's point of view, it was in many ways too general. For example, it contained no recipes for the pancakes, wafers, seed cakes, pasties, and frumenty that he recommended to her for use on such special occasions as Shrove Tuesday, sheepshearing, or harvest home.

Unless she was illiterate or unusually shiftless, the homemaker of course had her own written collection of receipts, medicinal as well as culinary, gathered from family and friends. A surprising number of early English manuscript receipt books, many of them beautifully written, have survived and can now be found in such collections as the Bitting in the Library of Congress and the Whitney in the New York Public Library.[3] Or the well-to-do mistress of a household might own one of the rather few works on cookery printed in England before 1600, such as the several very rare items now in the Whitney collection.[4]

After Gervase Markham's popular works began dispensing their widely inclusive advice, the seventeenth-century wife might find that her sporting husband's copy of Markham's *Countrey Contentments* included, in addition, *The English Huswife: Containing the Inward and Outward Vertues which ought to be in a Complete Woman.*[5] For the housewife's exclusive use, the latter section was frequently bound separately. Or it was combined with Markham's *English Husbandman* to make an extremely desirable reference work. It would be interesting to know how many copies of these two popular works were worn past preserving in colonial homes. We do know from the records of the Virginia Company of London that as early as 1620, copies of the two "bound togeather" were destined for use in America.[6]

Markham's *English Huswife*, besides containing a lengthy section devoted to cookery, which began with a calendar for planting necessary herbs in the right phases of the moon, also gave explicit advice about dairying and brewing; on making hempen, linen, and woolen cloth; and on how to achieve "vertue in physick," which covered everything from remedies for "griefes in stomacke" and an ointment to "breede haire" to cures for consumption and the plague. As for the inward virtues the housewife ought to possess, these, too, covered a wide field. They ranged from being religious to being witty, from being chaste of thought to being "wise in discourse but not frequent therein." Save that Markham's book lacked candlemaking instructions, the English housewife could scarcely have wished for a work better calculated to guide her in all her activities. The colonial wife, on the other hand, would come to feel that the work had certain lacunae. In America she had learned to use native_materials, the butternut in her dye pot, for example. But until a more specifically American work could be written, a book like Markham's was invaluable to her.

The success of Markham's publications encouraged many another author eager to advise on household affairs. The seventeenth century saw a marked increase in the number of such works printed in England. "Cabinets" and "Closets," including Queen Henrietta Maria's, were opened to disclose receipts for cookery, confectionery, distilling, "physick," and "chirgurie." [7] Moreover, women entered the field as authors when the Countess of Kent's *True Gentlewoman's Delight* and Hannah Woolley's *Queenlike Closet* were published. [8]

The next century produced an almost overwhelming number of English works embracing the art of cookery. Many were the product of women writers, and an increasing proportion dealt exclusively with cooking. The varieties offered were numerous: queen's, royal, court, England's new, modern, complete, professed, easy, and economical. The cooks whom the works were intended to suit were characterized by even more diverse adjectives: British, English, London, court, country, universal, modern, complete, family, pastry, experienced, prudent, frugal, and accomplished. A colonial bookseller thus had a wealth of titles from which he might choose to please his growing clientele.

But long as was the list from which she might select, the needs of the eighteenth-century American housewife could not be completely met by any one of the British works. Colonial cookery had undergone numerous changes since her ancestors had first established homes in the New World, and British authors seemed unaware of the resulting American needs in cooking instructions.

It was a noteworthy event, therefore, when the first edition of Amelia Simmons's *American Cookery* appeared in Hartford, Connecticut, in the spring of 1796. [9] So far as we know this was the first cookbook of American authorship to be published in the United

States. The work was an unpretentious volume, paper covered, and of only forty-seven octavo pages. Its contents lived up to its straight-forward title: the receipts it contained and its section on "Catering, or the Procuring the Best Viands, Fish, &c" recorded the changes that had taken place in our cookery and even in our speech. More-over, the inclusion of many of these American variations marked their first appearance in print. Consequently, Amelia Simmons's work was, in its minor sphere, another declaration of American independence.

Credit should in fairness be given to an earlier attempt to publish a cookbook particularly suited to American users. William Parks, printer at Williamsburg, was the innovator. When he published his edition of E. Smith's *Compleat Housewife* in 1742, he did so with the stated purpose of excluding receipts, "The Ingredients or Materi-als for which, are not to be had in this Country." [10] Such things as skirrets and broom buds apparently fell within that category. In so far as he followed his guiding principle of including only such receipts as were "useful and practicable here," the cookery section of Parks's book might also be labeled "American." But this negative approach could not mirror, as Amelia Simmons's book did, the changes that Americans had been making in their cookery.

During the following half century or so several other standard British works were reprinted in America. Notable are two editions of Carter's *The Frugal Housewife*, the first of which (Boston, 1772) has plates on carving by Paul Revere, and Briggs's almost encyclo-pedic *The New Art of Cookery*.[11] The largest of these leather-bound volumes ran to 557 pages, but none even claimed to be par-ticularly concerned with American tastes, ingredients, or necessities.

Little is known of Amelia Simmons. She was, she said, an Ameri-can orphan, and her preface reveals a preoccupation with that status in life. She described herself as one "circumscribed in her knowledge" and without "an education sufficient to prepare the work for the press," a fact that was to cause her some distress. The enterprise seems to have been her own, for the title page announced that the printing, done by Hudson and Goodwin, was "For the Author," a practice by no means universal. That she was a down-to-earth person, shrewd and practical, we can scarcely doubt. Her work, being without an expensive binding, could—and did—sell for 2s. 3d., a price which justified its purchase even in homes where the family income would permit the buying of little printed matter besides the yearly almanac. Her material was a well-calculated combination of the most common and practical recipes and those suited to special occasions and to more liberal food allowances. The book thus made an appeal to a wide audience and came close to justifying her claim that it was adapted "to all Grades of Life."

Many of her receipts were outright borrowings from British cookery books of the period, particularly Susannah Carter's. But this plagiarism was then—and even much later—accepted as customary procedure. She too was to suffer from such practices, even though her work was covered—apparently not very effectively—by the first Federal copyright law, of 1790. Based on standard works, her book contained the expected and traditional directions for making meat pies, trifles, and syllabubs, and instructions on how "To Dress a Turtle." The originality of Amelia Simmons's work lies in its recognition that an American could not find in a British cookbook recipes for making dishes that she as an American had known and eaten all her life. The deficiencies of British works stemmed largely from one source: Americans used ingredients that Europeans did not ordinarily employ. Amelia Simmons was the first writer of cookery books to set to work with that fact in mind.

Modern Americans who learn in kindergarten the importance of Indian corn to our colonial life will find it hard to believe that it took almost two centuries for a recipe treating this common ingredient to find its way into a cookery book. But British authors, having had no experience with its use, did not recognize the existence of this New World grain. Amelia Simmons demonstrated her practicality and proved that her work was truly "Adapted to this Country" by including five receipts requiring the use of corn meal: three for Indian Pudding, one for "Johny Cake or Hoe Cake," and one for "Indian Slapjacks." This was the first known appearance of any of the three in any cookbook.

Other recipes, too, mark this work as original and as plainly the product of an American cook—the inclusion of "Pompkin" Puddings, for example. British works of the day included many varieties of pudding, and the pumpkin was known in Europe, but previous American cookery imprints had not employed this ingredient. Actually, Amelia Simmons's pumpkin puddings would be called "pies" in America today. They were baked in crusts, and the ingredients of the filling were similar to those used in present-day pumpkin pie. This is not to say that Americans were then without a dish called "pumpkin pie." Mrs. Silvester Gardiner of Boston set down the rules for one in her book marked "Receipts from 1763." [12] However, this pie was made by placing alternate layers of raw apple and raw pumpkin, both sliced and well sugared, under a crust. The baked result was similar to deep-dish apple pie and very different from what we now know as pumpkin pie. By 1796, in Amelia Simmons's work, eggs, cream, sugar, and spice were being mixed with stewed pumpkin to create what has become an American Thanksgiving Day classic.

Her "Crookneck, or Winter Squash Pudding" was another newcomer to cookery books. Here even the word "squash" was an American contribution. Nor was this word the only borrowing from the American Indian that the recipe revealed. A practice learned from him was copied when she suggested that "dry whortleberries scattered in, will make it better."

Another noteworthy innovation was the inclusion of the Jerusalem artichoke among the book's "Directions for . . . Procuring the Best Viands, Fish, &c." This North American root had been introduced into England early in the seventeenth century, where it had at first been received as "dainties for a Queene," according to John Parkinson, herbarist to Charles I. But in 1629, when his herbal appeared, Parkinson had to report also that in his country the vegetable's "being so plentifull and cheape, hath rather bred a loathing then a liking of them." [13] British cookbooks reflected this distaste. Even Briggs's voluminous work did not contain a recipe for cooking them. *American Cookery* did, marking again the beginning of a divergence in the cookery books of the two peoples.

Finally, the work introduced another novelty American cookbooks were to copy—a recipe "For brewing Spruce Beer." This beverage had also been overlooked by British-American imprints on cookery. Long revered in Europe and America as an antiscorbutic, spruce beer had been much used on long sailing voyages and by armies on both sides of the Atlantic. The decoction, especially when fermented by the use of molasses, was recommended by the Scottish doctor James Lind in his *Treatise of the Scurvy* in 1753.[14] Perhaps faith in the remedy persisted longer on this side of the water, or perhaps the greater availability of spruce caused the inclusion of the recipe in Amelia Simmons's work. Certainly her book set a fashion for many American cookery books. Additions made to the New York edition of Carter's *Frugal Housewife* in 1803 included an "Appendix containing Several New Receipts Adapted to the American Mode of Cooking" where two recipes for brewing this beer were to be found.[15]

In minor details, Amelia Simmons's work was equally American. Corn cobs were used in the smoking of bacon; her roast turkey receipt called for accompanying "cramberry-sauce"; she used watermelon rinds to make "American citron"; and her directions for treating "Minced Pies" reflected the New England custom of long-range pie baking: "Weeks after, when you have occasion to use them, carefully raise the top crust, and with a round edg'd spoon, collect the meat into a bason, which warm with additional wine and spices to the taste of your circle, while the crust is also warm'd like a hoe cake, put carefully together and serve up, by this means you can have hot pies through the winter, and enrich'd singly to your company."

Thus far we have seen characteristics of *American Cookery* that have remained rather exclusively American, if they have survived at all. In addition, the work recorded an innovation that was to revolutionize European cookery as well. This novelty was the introduction of chemical leaven into doughs, a practice which was to result in the compounding of modern baking powders. Until nearly the end of the eighteenth century, the desired lightness in baked goods was produced by beating in air along with eggs, or adding yeast or various spirits to produce a ferment. Even cakes were leavened with yeast. But by 1796, someone—and the evidence seems to point to an anonymous American woman—had dared to introduce a chemical into her dough to produce carbon dioxide in a hurry. Joseph Priestley had already shown the world how to carbonate water, but the materials he had used were acid and wet chalk.[16] In America, cooks of Amelia Simmons's time were adding pearlash to gingerbread and cooky doughs, and her work is the first cookbook known to have recommended the ingredient.

This newcomer to the oven was a well-known staple of American households where soap was a homemade article and where wool was scoured or cloth bleached. In all these processes, as well as in the manufacture of glass, potash or its refined form, pearlash, was a desired ingredient. Consequently, the European who lacked the forests from which these ashes were procured had made "sope ashes" one of the products to be sought in America. The extent of their manufacture here in the late 1790's just when their use in baking was becoming common, is recorded in the account that the Duc de La Rochefoucauld-Liancourt wrote of his travels in the United States in the years 1795 to 1797. At Albany and "other American cities, the back country of which has been lately cleared," he found the ashes "forming a considerable branch of the trade," for in addition to the quantities used locally, the annual amount leaving United States harbors had reached close to 8,000 tons in 1792.[17] It is hard to imagine an American housewife unfamiliar with these "cheap and plentiful"[18] ingredients when Amelia Simmons's cookbook appeared.

That the use of these ashes in baking was an American innovation seems established by the publicity given the method in 1799 when it apparently first became known in England. In the United States, controversy had arisen over the comparative merits of alkalis and acids, a discussion which incidentally led to the question whether potash, "which women have [for] so great a duration of time mingled with their cakes,"[19] was wholesome for children. The debate evoked two letters from Dr. Samuel Latham Mitchill, a professor at Columbia College, and these letters, first circulated in New York, were then published in the London *Monthly Magazine* in early 1799. Their appearance excited an inquiry from a British reader about the cakes "and the manner of making them."[20] An explanatory letter from a Long Island woman was lengthy and detailed.[21] The fact that the

British magazine gave more than two pages to her discussion of a cake leaven suggests that the method was still a novelty in Britain. Yet, in early 1796 *American Cookery* contained four recipes, two for cookies and two for gingerbread, requiring this forerunner of baking powder.[22]

The portion of Amelia Simmons's *American Cookery* devoted to gingerbread revealed another emerging American preference. For centuries, gingerbread had been a traditional European pastry, a thin, flat, spiced confection similar to what we call a cooky today and eminently suited to the making of gingerbread men. To achieve the desired result, the dough was rolled thin and cut or printed in molds. "This is your Gingerbread used at the Court, and in all gentlemens houses at festival times," wrote Sir Hugh Plat of similar pastry in the early seventeenth century.[23] More than 150 years later the receipts in the manuscript cookbook used by Martha Washington were for this same kind of gingerbread. "Prints is moste used after the second course in christmas," says one of her receipts; and another, "The prints of white ginger bread are used much thinner then the cullerd which is commonly made allmoste halfe an Intch thick or a quarter of an intch at the least."[24] There can be little doubt that the kind of gingerbread that figured as a refreshment for troops on early mustering days and quasimartial occasions was of this same cooky-like, convenient variety. "We ate gingerbread all day long and saw the Governor exercise the foot," wrote William Byrd of Westover while with his troops in a display of strength calculated to intimidate the Tuscarora Indians in 1711.[25] And the gingerbread bought by the seventeen-year-old Benjamin Franklin on his way to Philadelphia was almost certainly no other kind.[26] Amelia Simmons's work contained recipes for this popular and easily vendible type of pastry, but it also contained a recipe called "Soft Gingerbread to be baked in pans," the ancestor of the cake-like baked product that usually comes to the American mind when the word "gingerbread" is mentioned. Moreover, so far as we have been able to discover, this was the first time the recipe appeared in American print.

Amelia Simmons's section on gingerbread illustrates another

point, her choice of language. When she called one variety "Molasses Gingerbread," she was voicing the American preference for the use of this word over the "treacle" of British recipes like those of E. Smith. Several other words testify to the fact that she wrote in the vernacular. Her use of the Americanism "emptins,"[27] a colloquial variation of "emptyings," is particularly striking. This word had first been applied to the lees of beer, cider, or wine, specifically when these dregs were used as a ferment; only later was it applied to the semi-liquid prepared yeast so commonly used in the baking of bread even long after Amelia Simmons's day. Her use of the term is extremely early; the first citation noted in the *Dictionary of American English* is one of 1839. Moreover, two Americanisms, "slapjack" for a cake fried on a griddle and "Hannah Hill" for the sea bass,[28] appeared here thirteen and eighteen years earlier, respectively, than their first uses claimed by the same dictionary. Amelia Simmons also used the word "shortning"—in later editions corrected to "shortening"—to denote fats, specifying that the proportions she used were "half butter and half lard.[29] "Shortening" has been curiously slighted in works devoted to the history of words. The *Dictionary of American English* does not include it, nor do we find Mencken interested in its origins. The *New English Dictionary* cites the date of its first printed appearance in Britain as 1823, when it was listed in a work on Suffolk words. Yet Amelia Simmons used it as a term familiar to Americans in 1796. By 1828, it had become so well established in our vocabulary that Webster included it in his *American Dictionary of the English Language.*[30]

American Cookery was also the first American cookbook to use two words that we have borrowed from the Dutch: "cooky" and "slaw."[31] The former is from *"koekje,"* the Dutch name for what British cookbooks called "cakes" or "little cakes." In colonial New York *koekjes* were a popular treat offered to New Year's Day callers, and English-speaking New Yorkers took over the name as well as the custom. How easily this word became Americanized is illustrated by the Revolutionary diary of Jabez Fitch from Connecticut, taken prisoner on Long Island. Fitch's phonetic spelling wavered all the way from "fregize" to "friggarzie" when he wanted to write "fricassee," but *koekjes* became "cookies" on the first try.[32] The Americanism appeared in print in the New York *Daily Advertiser* in 1786,[33] so Amelia Simmons's use of it was not new or original. However, her work was the first American cookbook to abandon the British name for the pastry. "Slaw" for the Dutch *"sla,"* meaning salad, had also been in the process of absorption into our vocabulary for quite a period of time.[34] When the two words appeared in *American Cookery,* they were still very much in the vernacular, however: though Webster had accepted "shortening" by 1828, "cooky" and "slaw" were still unrecognized by him.[35]

Just as an internal examination of Amelia Simmons's *American Cookery* reveals a break with earlier efforts to meet the needs of American cooks, so an external examination—of its publishing history—suggests the degree of its influence on other works. The Connecticut District Court issued a copyright to Amelia Simmons on April 28, 1796.[36] A copy of her work was deposited on May 26 of that year in the office of the Secretary of State in Washington, who was then the custodian of such volumes.[37] On June 8, Isaac Beers of New Haven announced in the *Connecticut Journal* that the book was just published and was to be sold by him. It was a large advertisement for a single book to receive in those days, for its full title required space: *American Cookery, or the Art of Dressing Viands, Fish, Poultry and Vegetables, and the Best Modes of Making Pastes, Puffs, Pies, Tarts, Puddings, Custards and Preserves, and All Kinds of Cakes, from the Imperial Plumb to Plain Cake. Adapted to this Country, and All Grades of Life. By Amelia Simmons, an American Orphan.* During August and September an advertisement that *American Cookery* was "For Sale at this Office" appeared in seven consecutive issues of the weekly *Middlesex Gazette* published in Middletown, Connecticut.[38] As this was a busy market center to which farmers from New York, Massachusetts, New Hampshire, and Vermont brought cattle for export to the West Indies, it is probable that the book had considerable distribution from this source in the saddlebags of home-faring drovers.

Two different versions of the 1796 edition appeared, both of them now exceedingly rare, though the durable rag paper upon which they were printed prepared them to withstand hard usage. The second[39] is supplemented by a sheet of obviously dissimilar paper on which is printed the following "Advertisement": "The author of the American Cookery, not having an education sufficient to prepare the work for the press, the person that was employed by her, and entrusted with the receipts, to prepare them for publication, (with a design to impose on her, and injure the sale of the book) did omit several articles very essential in some of the receipts, and placed others in their stead, which were highly injurious to them, without her consent—which was unknown to her, till after publication; but she has removed them as far as possible, by the following Errata." The appended corrections do indeed cover some serious errors such as the omission of flour for thickening puddings and the doubling of the amount of "emptins" required to leaven a cake. Unfortunately for the users of her books as well as for Amelia Simmons's reputation, her attempts at rectification never completely caught up with the printings of her original recipes.

If we can believe her own statement about the success of the first edition, the demand had "been so great, and the sale so rapid" that she found herself "under a necessity of publishing a second edition." This she did in Albany, probably in 1800.[40] It was an extensively revised and considerably augmented work. There were new recipes such as "Election Cake" (beginning with thirty quarts of flour), "Independence Cake," and "Federal Pan Cake," recording by their names America's awareness of its new status as a nation. The new edition also contained a recipe for "Chouder," already an accepted part of the American menu and previously in print, and a recipe requiring the use of that very American combination of rye flour and corn meal, "rye 'n' injun."

The second edition was widely reprinted, with only slight omissions; first at some undesignated place; then at Walpole, New Hampshire; twice at Brattleboro, Vermont; and in New York at Poughkeepsie.[41] Some of these were possibly unauthorized, for Amelia Simmons's name did not appear on the title page. Finally, two different augmented versions were published in New York City and Woodstock, Vermont, the latter in 1831.[42] The original version, also, made two later appearances, both bearing her name and both carrying the mistakes she had tried to correct.[43]

All these editions and printings of Amelia Simmons's work, whether or not they carried her name, were made under the original title. But *American Cookery* was also published under disguised names. *New American Cookery . . . By an American Lady,* published in New York in 1805, was a complete word-for-word reprint of Amelia Simmons's revised edition minus her prefaces and with some material added.[44] *The New-England Cookery . . . Compiled by Lucy Emerson,* which appeared in Montpelier, Vermont, three years later,[45] was a less flagrant plagiarism, for it disclaimed "pretensions to the originality of the whole of the receipts herein contained." However, it was largely a reprint of the first and uncorrected edition of *American Cookery*. The final plagiarism was perhaps the worst: Harriet Whiting's *Domestic Cookery* published in Boston in 1819 contained no recipe that had not appeared in the original work of Amelia Simmons, and exactly as it was then printed.[46] Harriet Whiting did not, however, claim to be an orphan, nor did she bother to correct the recipes.

For thirty-five years, then, between the time of her first edition in 1796 and the Woodstock edition of 1831, Amelia Simmons's awareness of a distinctly American cookery had an impact directly upon the contents of American culinary imprints. Meanwhile, her book was affecting other cookbooks. Editors of British works about to be published in America acknowledged the validity of her assumption and took steps to compete with her work.

Susannah Carter's *Frugal Housewife,*[47] Hannah Glasse's *The Art of Cookery Made Plain and Easy,*[48] and Maria Rundell's *A New System of Domestic Cookery,*[49] all bowed in the direction of the American cook and, incidentally, in the direction of Amelia Simmons. Pumpkin pie, spruce beer, doughnuts, crullers, waffles, maple beer, maple molasses, squash, corn meal, and clams made their way into these new editions of old works. Claims of being adapted to the "American Mode of Cooking" or to the use of "Private Families Throughout the United States" advertised these new culinary wares.

While all cookbooks subsequently printed in America were not adapted to specifically American requirements,[50] a fact for which we may be grateful, a pattern had been established, a model created, by Amelia Simmons in 1796. *American Cookery* was eventually superseded, and many another American woman's name appeared on the title page of a book on cooking. In time, the awareness of indigenous cookery extended even to geographical differences, and regional works began to appear. But Amelia Simmons still holds her place as the mother of American cookery books. And no later work, however completely it may reflect the mores of this country, has quite the freshness of this first glimpse caught in the small mirror held up by an American Orphan.

NOTES

---

[1] Richard Standfast, *A Little Handful of Cordial Comforts for Fainting Souls; Intended Chiefly for the Good of Those that Walk Mournfully with God* (Boston, 1690).

[2] Thomas Tusser, *Five Hundreth Pointes of Good Husbandrie . . . Also a Table of Husbandrie . . . and Another of Huswiferie . . .* (London, 1593).

[3] See Katherine Golden Bitting, *Gastronomic Bibliography* (San Francisco, 1939), for the asterisked items which were in her own collection, now in the Library of Congress, and Lewis M. Stark, "The Whitney Cookery Collection," New York Public Library, *Bulletin*, L (1946), 103-126.

[4] Thomas Dawson, *The Good Huswifes Jewell . . .* (London, 1587); *A Book of Cookrye . . . Gathered by A. W. . . . .* (London, 1587); and *The Good Hous-wives Treasurie . . .* (London, 1588).

[5] Gervase Markham, *Countrey Contentments, in two Bookes: . . . the Second Intituled, The English Huswife: Containing the Inward and Outward Vertues which ought to be in a Compleate Woman: as her Phisicke, Cookery, Banqueting-stuffe, Distillation, Perfumes, Wooll, Hemp, Flaxe, Dairies, Brewing, Baking, and all other Things Belonging to an Houshold . . .* (London, 1615).

[6] *The Records of the Virginia Company of London*, ed. Susan M. Kingsbury, 4 vols. (Washington, 1906-1935), III, 389. The notation reads: "ffor markams worke of husbandry & huswifry bound togeather and for the like of Gowges &c." The "like of Gowges" was probably one of Conrad Heresbach's works which Barnaby Googe "Englished and increased," as, in one edition, under the title *The Whole Art and Trade of Husbandry Contained in Four Bookes . . .* (London, 1614).

[7] Hugh Plat, *A Closet for Ladies and Gentlewomen . . .* (London, 1630); Lord Patrick Ruthven, *The Ladies Cabinet Enlarged and Opened . . .* (London, 1654); and *The Queens Closet Opened . . . Transcribed . . . by W. M., one of her late Servants . . .* (London, 1656).

[8] Elizabeth Grey, Countess of Kent, *A True Gentlewoman's Delight, Wherein is Contained all Manner of Cookery* . . . (London, 1659); and Hannah Woolley, *The Queen-like Closet: or, Rich Cabinet, Stored with all Manner of Rare Receipts for Preserving, Candying and Cookery* . . . , 5th ed. (London, 1684).

[9] Amelia Simmons, *American Cookery, or the Art of Dressing Viands, Fish, Poultry and Vegetables, and the Best Modes of Making Pastes, Puffs, Pies, Tarts, Puddings, Custards and Preserves, and All Kinds of Cakes, from the Imperial Plumb to Plain Cake. Adapted to this Country, and All Grades of Life. By Amelia Simmons, an American Orphan. Published According to Act of Congress* (Hartford, Conn., 1796).

[10] E. [Eliza?] Smith, *The Compleat Housewife; or, Accomplish'd Gentlewoman's Companion . . . Collected from the Fifth Edition* (Williamsburg, Va., 1742).

[11] Susannah Carter, *The Frugal Housewife, or Complete Woman Cook* . . . (Boston, [1772]; New York, [ca. 1792]); Richard Briggs, *The New Art of Cookery, According to the Present Practice* . . . (Philadelphia, 1792).

[12] Anne (Gibbons) Gardiner, *Mrs. Gardiner's Receipts from 1763* (Hallowell, Me., 1938), p. 76.

[13] John Parkinson, *Paradisi In Sole Paradisus Terrestris. Or a Garden of All Sorts of Pleasant Flowers . . . with a Kitchen Garden of all Manner of Herbes, Rootes, & Fruites, for Meate or Sause Used with Us* . . . (London, 1629), p. 518.

[14] James Lind, *A Treatise of the Scurvy* (Edinburgh, 1753), pp. 222-223.

[15] S. Carter, *The Frugal Housewife . . . To Which is Added an Appendix, Containing Several New Receipts Adapted to the American Mode of Cooking* (New York, 1803), p. 212.

[16] Joseph Priestley, *Directions for Impregnating Water with Fixed Air* . . . (London, 1772), pp. 7-9.

[17] François-Alexandre-Frédéric, Duc de La Rochefoucauld-Liancourt, *Travels through the United States . . . in the Years 1795, 1796, and 1797* . . . , 2d ed., 4 vols. (London, 1800), I, 225; II, 56, 84-88, 211; III, 313, 381, 441; IV, facing 448.

[18] Said particularly of potash: *Monthly Magazine*, VIII (1799), 875.

[19] *Ibid.*, VII (1799), 195.

[20] *Ibid.*, VII, 108-110, 194-195, 380. It is interesting to note that the first English translation of Lavoisier that was made specifically for an American audience was of his work on potashes. See Denis I. Duveen and Herbert S. Klickstein, "The 'American' Edition of Lavoisier's *L'art de fabriquer le salin et la potasse*," *William and Mary Quarterly*, 3d Ser., XIII (1956), 493-498.

[21] *Monthly Mag.*, VIII, 873-875.

[22] Simmons, *American Cookery*, pp. 35-36. Support for the idea that the use of the ashes in baking was an American innovation is to be found by comparing two editions of a volume by the lawyer-agriculturist John Beale Bordley of Philadelphia. When his *Essays and Notes on Husbandry and Rural Affairs* was published (Philadelphia, 1799), its section on "Diet in Rural Economy" contained cookery recipes gleaned from many British sources. None employed either potash or pearlash. However, the second edition of the *Essays* contained a condensed version of the very recipe that had been published in the *Monthly Magazine*. It is hard to escape the conclusion that the earlier work would have contained the recipe had it then been known in England. When he did publish his directions for what he called "Handy-Cake or Bread," Bordley's added comment probably helped to popularize the new leaven: "The potash or salt of tartar is most excellent for health, especially of people apt to be affected with slow or bilious fevers, in flat countries." See Bordley, *Essays and Notes . . . Second Edition with Additions* (Philadelphia, 1801), pp. 411-412.

[23] Sir Hugh Plat, *Delightes for Ladies . . .* (London, 1948), p. 30.

[24] Martha Washington's MS "A Booke of Sweetmeats," Receipts nos. 188, 189, Historical Society of Pennsylvania library.

[25] William Byrd, *The Secret Diary of William Byrd of Westover, 1709-1712*, ed. Louis B. Wright and Marion Tinling (Richmond, 1941), p. 423.

[26] Benjamin Franklin, *Autobiography*, Everyman's Library (New York, 1931), p. 29.

[27] Simmons, *American Cookery*, pp. 33, 35-38.

[28] *Ibid.*, pp. 34, 6.

[29] *Ibid.*, pp. 34-35.

[30] Noah Webster, *An American Dictionary of the English Language . . .* (New York, 1828).

[31] Simmons, *American Cookery*, pp. 35, 14.

[32] Jabez Fitch, *The New-York Diary of Lieutenant Jabez Fitch . . .* , ed. W. H. W. Sabine (New York, 1954), pp. 82, 89, 93, 174.

[33] *The Daily Advertiser: Political, Historical, and Commercial,* New York, Mar. 20, 1786.

[34] It, too, had been recorded in Fitch's *Diary* during May 1777, p. 173.

[35] Webster, *American Dictionary*.

[36] Charles Evans, *An American Bibliography . . .* , 13 vols. (Chicago and Worcester, Mass., 1903-1955), XI, 55.

[37] MS Records of Department of State. Registers of Copyrights Received, 1796-1842, I, Library of Congress.

[38] *Middlesex Gazette,* Middletown, Conn., Aug. 5 to Sept. 16, 1796.

[39] The American Antiquarian Society copy reproduced here.

[40] A. Simmons, *American Cookery . . . The Second Edition* (Albany, [ca. 1800]).

[41] [A. Simmons], *American Cookery . . . By an American Orphan* (n. p., 1808), (Walpole, N. H., 1812), (Brattleboro Vt., 1814 and 1819), and (Poughkeepsie, N. Y., 1815).

[42] *Ibid.* (New York, 1822); *American Cookery . . . Together with Rules of Carving at Dinner Parties. Exemplified with Cuts. By an Orphan. 2d Edition Improved* (Woodstock, Vt., 1831).

[43] A. Simmons, *American Cookery . . .* (Hartford, Conn., 1798) and (Troy, N. Y., 1808).

[44] *New American Cookery, or Female Companion . . . Peculiarly Adapted to the American Mode of Cooking. By an American Lady* (New York, 1805).

[45] Lucy Emerson, *The New-England Cookery . . . Particularly Adapted to this Part of our Country . . .* (Montpelier, Vt., 1808).

[46] Harriet Whiting, *Domestic Cookery, or the Art of Dressing Viands, Fish, Poultry and Vegetables; and the Best Modes of Making Pastes, . . . and All Kinds of Cakes from the Imperial Plum to Plain Cake* (Boston, 1819).

[47] See above, note 15.

[48] Hannah Glasse, *The Art of Cookery Made Plain and Easy . . . A New Edition, with Modern Improvements* (Alexandria, Va., 1805), pp. 137-144.

[49] [Maria Eliza (Ketelby) Rundell], *A New System of Domestic Cookery . . . Adapted to the Use of Private Families Throughout the United States* (New York, 1814).

[50] See, for examples, Elizabeth Raffald, *The Experienced English Housekeeper, for the Use and Ease of Ladies, Housekeepers, Cooks, &c. . . . A New Edition* (Philadelphia, 1818); Louis Eustache Ude, *The French Cook* (Philadelphia, 1828).

THE
FIRST AMERICAN
COOKBOOK

AMERICAN COOKERY,

OR THE ART OF DRESSING

VIANDS, FISH, POULTRY and VEGETABLES,

AND THE BEST MODES OF MAKING

PASTES, PUFFS, PIES, TARTS, PUDDINGS, CUSTARDS AND PRESERVES,

AND ALL KINDS OF

C A K E S,

FROM THE IMPERIAL PLUMB TO PLAIN CAKE.

ADAPTED TO THIS COUNTRY,

AND ALL GRADES OF LIFE.

By Amelia Simmons,

AN AMERICAN ORPHAN.

PUBLISHED ACCORDING TO ACT OF CONGRESS.

HARTFORD

PRINTED BY HUDSON & GOODWIN.

FOR THE AUTHOR.

1796

PREFACE.

✦✦✦✦✦✦✦✦✦✦✦✦✦

AS this treatife is calculated for the improvement of the rifing generation of *Females* in America, the Lady of fafhion and fortune will not be difpleafed, if many hints are fuggefted for the more general and univerfal knowledge of thofe females in this country, who by the lofs of their parents, or other unfortunate circumftances, are reduced to the neceffity of going into families in the line of domeftics, or taking refuge with their friends or relations, and doing thofe things which are really effential to the perfecting them as good wives, and ufeful members of fociety. The orphan, tho' left to the care of virtuous guardians, will find it effentially neceffary to have an opinion and determination of her own. The world, and the fafhion thereof, is fo variable, that old people cannot accommodate themfelves to the various changes and fafhions which daily occur ; *they* will adhere to the fafhion of *their* day, and will not furrender their attachments to the *good old way*—while the young and the gay, bend and conform readily to the tafte of the times, and fancy of the hour. By having an opinion and determination, I would not be underftood to mean an obftinate perfeverance in trifles, which borders on obftinacy—by no means, but only an adherence to thofe rules and maxims which have ftood the teft of ages, and will forever eftablifh the *female character*, a virtuous character—altho' they conform to the ruling tafte of the age in cookery, drefs, language, manners, &c.

PREFACE.

It muft ever remain a check upon the poor folita-
ry orphan, that while thofe females who have parents, or brothers, or riches, to defend their indif-
cretions, that the orphan muft depend folely upon
character. How immenfely important, therefore,
that every action, every word, every thought, be re-
gulated by the ftricteft purity, and that every movement meet the approbation of the good and wife.

The candor of the American Ladies is folicitoufly
intreated by the Authorefs, as fhe is circumfcribed in
her knowledge, this being an original work in this
country.   Should any future editions appear, fhe
hopes to render it more valuable.

DIRECTIONS for CATERING, or the procuring the beſt VIANDS, FISH, &c.

How to chooſe Fleſh.

BEEF. The large ſtall fed ox beef is the beſt, it has a coarſe open grain, and oily ſmoothneſs ; dent it with your finger and it will immediately riſe again ; if old, it will be rough and ſpungy, and the dent remain.

Cow Beef is leſs boned, and generally more tender and juicy than the ox, in America, which is uſed to labor.

Of almoſt every ſpecies of Animals, Birds and Fiſhes, the female is the tendereſt, the richeſt flavour'd, and among poultry the ſooneſt fatened.

Mutton, grafs-fed, is good two or three years old.

Lamb, if under ſix months is rich, and no danger of impoſition ; it may be known by its ſize, in diſtinguiſhing either.

Veal, is foon loſt—great care therefore is neceſſary in purchaſing. Veal bro't to market in panniers, or in carriages, is to be prefered to that bro't in bags, and flouncing on a ſweaty horſe.

Pork, is known by its ſize, and whether properly fattened by its appearance.

To make the beſt Bacon.

To each ham put one ounce ſaltpetre, one pint bay ſalt, one pint molaſſes, ſhake together 6 or 8 weeks, or when a large quantity is together, baſt them with the liquor every day ; when taken out to dry, fmoke three weeks with cobs or malt fumes. To every ham may be added a cheek, if you ftow away a barrel and not alter the compofition, fome add a fhoulder. For tranfportation or exportation, double the period of fmoaking.

Fiſh, how to chooſe the beſt in market.

Salmon, the nobleſt and richeſt fiſh taken in freſh water—the largeſt are the beſt. They are unlike al-moſt every other fiſh, are ameliorated by being 3 or 4 days out of water, if kept from heat and the moon, which has much more injurious effeēt than the fun.

In all great fiſh-markets, great fiſh-mongers ſtriētly examine the gills—if the bright redneſs is exchang-ed for a low brown, they are ſtale ; but when live fiſh are bro't flouncing into market, you have only to eleēt the kind moſt agreeable to your palate and the feafon.

Shad, contrary to the generally received opinion are not fo much richer flavored, as they are harder when firſt taken out of the water ; opinions vary ref-peēting them. I have taſted Shad thirty or forty miles from the place where caught, and really con-ceived that they had a richneſs of flavor, which did not appertain to thofe taken freſh and cooked imme-diately, and have proved both at the fame table, and the truth may reſt here, that a Shad 36 or 48 hours out of water, may not cook fo hard and folid, and be efteemedfo elegant, yet give a higher reliſhed flavor to the taſte.

Every fpecies generally of *falt water Fiſh,* are beſt freſh from the water, tho' the *Hannah Hill, Black Fiſh, Lobſter, Oyſter, Flounder, Baſs, Cod, Haddock,* and *Eel,* with many others, may be tranfported by land many miles, find a good market, and retain a good reliſh ; but as generally, live ones are bought firſt, deceits are ufed to give them a freſhneſs of ap-pearance, fuch as peppering the gills, wetting the fins and tails, and even painting the gills, or wetting with

animal blood. Experience and attention will dictate
the choice of the beſt. Freſh gills, full bright eyes,
moiſt fins and tails, are denotements of their being
freſh caught ; if they are ſoft, its certain they are
ſtale, but if deceits are uſed, your ſmell muſt approve
or denounce them, and be your ſafeſt guide.

Of all freſh water fiſh, there are none that require,
or ſo well afford haſte in cookery, as the *Salmon Trout*,
they are beſt when caught under a fall or cateract—
from what philoſophical circumſtance is yet unſettled,
yet true it is, that at the foot of a fall the waters are
much colder than at the head ; Trout chooſe thoſe
waters ; if taken from them and hurried into dreſs,
they are genuinely good ; and take rank in point of
ſuperiority of flavor, of moſt other fiſh.

Perch and Roach, are noble pan fiſh. the deeper
the water from whence taken, the finer are their fla-
vors ; if taken from ſhallow water, with muddy bottoms, they are impregnated therewith, and are un-
ſavory.

Eels, though taken from muddy bottoms, are beſt
to jump in the pan.

Moſt white or ſoft fiſh are beſt bloated, which is
done by ſalting, peppering, and drying in the ſun,
and in a chimney ; after 30 or 40 hours drying,
are beſt broiled, and moiſtened with butter, &c.

Poultry—how to chooſe.

Having before ſtated that the female in almoſt
every inſtance, is preferable to the male, and pecuﬂ-
arly ſo in the *Peacock*, which, tho' beautifully plum-
aged, is tough, hard, ſtringy, and untaſted, and even
indelicious—while the *Pea Hen* is exactly otherwiſe,
and the queen of all birds.

So alſo in a degree, *Turkey*.

Hen Turkey, is higher and richer flavor'd, eaſier
fattened and plumper—they are no odds in market.

Dunghill Fowls, are from their frequent uſe, a
tolerable proof of the former birds.

Chickens, of either kind are good, and the yellow leg'd the beft, and their tafte the fweeteft.

Capons, if young are good, are known by fhort fpurs and fmooth legs.

All birds are known, whether frefh killed or ftale, by a tight vent in the former, and a loofe open vent if old or ftale; their fmell denotes their goodnefs; fpeckled rough legs denote age, while fmooth legs and combs prove them young.

A Goofe, if young, the bill will be yellow, and will have but few hairs, the bones will crack eafily; but if old, the contrary, the bill will be red, and the pads ftill redder; the joints ftiff and difficultly disjointed; if young, otherwife; choofe one not very flefhy on the breaft, but fat in the rump.

Ducks, are fimilar to geefe.

Wild Ducks, have redder pads, and fmaller than the tame ones, otherwife are like the goofe or tame duck, or to be chofen by the fame rules.

Wood Cocks, ought to be thick, fat and flefh firm, the nofe dry, and throat clear.

Snipes, if young and fat, have full veins under the wing, and are fmall in the veins, otherwife like the Woodcock.

Partridges, if young, will have black bills, yellowifh legs; if old, the legs look bluifh; if old or ftale, it may be perceived by fmelling at their mouths.

Pigeons, young, have light red legs, and the flefh of a colour, and prick eafily—old have red legs, blackifh in parts, more hairs, plumper and loofe vents—fo alfo of grey or green Plover, Black Birds, Thrafh, Lark, and wild Fowl in general.

Hares, are white flefh'd and flexible when new and frefh kill'd; if ftale, their flefh will have a blackifh hue, like old pigions, if the cleft in her lip fpread much, is wide and ragged, fhe is old; the contrary when young.

Leveret, is like the Hare in every refpect, that

íome are obliged to fearch for the knob, or fmall bone on the fore leg or foot, to diftinguifh them.

Rabbits, the wild are the beft, either are good and tender ; if old there will be much yellowifh fat about the kidneys, the claws long, wool r ugh, and mixed with grey hairs ; if young the reverſe. As to their being frefh, judge by the ſcent, they foon perifh, if trap'd or fhot, and left in pelt or undreſſed ; their taint is quicker than veal, and the moſt fickifh in nature ; and will not, like beef or veal, be purged by fire.

The cultivation of Rabbits would be profitable in America, if the beft methods were purfued—they are a very prolific and profitable animal—they are eafily cultivated if properly attended, but not otherwife.— A Rabbit's borough, on which 3000 dollars may have been expended, might be very profitable ; but on the fmall fcale they would be well near market towns—eafier bred, and more valuable.

Butter—Tight, waxy, yellow Butter is better than white or crumbly, which foon becomes rancid and frowy. Go into the centre of balls or rolls to prove and judge it ; if in ferkin, the middle is to be preferred, as the fides are frequently diftafted by the wood of the firkin—altho' oak and ufed for years. New pine tubs are ruinous to the butter. To have fweet butter in dog days, and thro' the vegetable feafons, fend ſtone pots to honeft, neat, and trufty dairy people, and procure it pack'd down in May, and let them be brought in in the night. or cool rainy morning, covered with a clean cloth wet in cold water, and partake of no heat from the horfe, and fet the pots in the coldeft part of your cellar, or in the ice houfe.— Some fay that May butter thus preferved, will go into the winter ufe, better than fall made butter.

Cheefe—The red fmooth. moift coated, and tight preffed, fquare edged Cheefe, are better than white coat, hard rinded, or bilged ; the infide fhould be yellow, and flavored to your tafte. Old fhelves which have only been wiped down for years, are preferable to fcoured and wafhed fhelves. Deceits are ufed by falt-petering the out fide, or colouring with hemlock, cocumberries, or fafron, infufed into the milk ; the tafte of either fupercedes every poffible evafion.

Eggs—Clear, thin fhell'd, longeft oval and fharp ends are beft ; to afcertain whether new or ftale—hold to the light, if the white is clear, the yolk regularly in the centre, they are good—but if otherwife, they are ftale. The beft poffible method of afcertaining, is to put them into water, if they lye on their bilge, they are *good* and *frefh*—if they bob up an end they are ftale, and if they rife they are addled, proved, and of no ufe.

We proceed to ROOTS and VEGETABLES—*and the beft cook cannot alter the firft quality, they muft be good, or the cook will be difappointed.*

Potatoes, take rank for univerfal ufe, profit and eafy acquirement. The fmooth fkin, known by the name of How's Potatoe, is the moft mealy and richeft flavor'd ; the yellow rufticoat next beft ; the red, and red rufticoat are tolerable ; and the yellow Spanifh have their value—thofe cultivated from imported feed on fandy or dry loomy lands, are beft for table ufe ; tho' the red or either will produce more in rich, loomy, highly manured garden grounds ; new lands and a fandy foil, afford the richeft flavor'd ; and moft mealy Potatoe much depends on the ground on which they grow—more on the fpecies of Potatoes planted—and ftill more from foreign feeds—and each may be known by attention to connoiffeurs ; for a good potatoe comes up in many branches of cookery, as herein after prefcribed.—All potatoes fhould be dug before the rainy feafons in the fall, well dryed in the fun, kept from froft and dampnefs during the winter, in the fpring removed from the cellar to a dry loft, and fpread thin, and frequently ſtirred and dryed, or they will grow and be thereby injured for cookery.

A roaſt Potatoe is brought on with roaſt Beef, a Steake, a Chop, or Fricaſſee ; good boiled with a boiled diſh ; make an excellent ſtuffing for a turkey, water or wild fowl ; make a good pie, and a good ſtarch for many uſes. All potatoes run out, or depreciate in America ; a freſh importation of the Spaniſh might reſtore them to table uſe.

It would ſwell this treatiſe too much to ſay every thing that is uſeful, to prepare a good table, but I may be pardoned by obſerving, that the Iriſh have preſerved a genuine mealy rich Potatoe, for a century, which takes rank of any known in any other kingdom ; and I have heard that they renew their ſeed by planting and cultivating the *Seed Ball,* which grows on the tine. The manner of their managing it to keep up the excellency of that root, would better ſuit a treatiſe on agriculture and gardening than this—and be inſerted in a book which would be read by the farmer, inſtead of his amiable daughter. If no one treats on the ſubject, it may appear in the next edition.

Onions—The Medeira white is beſt in market, eſteemed ſofter flavored, and not ſo fiery, but the high red, round hard onions are the beſt ; if you conſult cheapneſs, the largeſt are beſt ; if you conſult taſte and ſoftneſs, the very ſmalleſt are the moſt delicate, and uſed at the firſt tables. Onions grow in the richeſt, higheſt cultivated ground, and better and better year after year, on the ſame ground.

Beets, grow on any ground, but beſt on loom, or light gravel grounds; the *red* is the richeſt and beſt approved ; the *white* has a ſickiſh ſweetneſs, which is diſliked by many.

Parſnips, are a valuable root, cultivated beſt in rich old grounds, and doubly deep plowed, *late ſown,* they grow thrifty, and are not ſo prongy ; they may be kept any where and any how, ſo that they do not grow with heat, or are nipped with froft; if frofted, let them thaw in earth ; they are richer flavored when plowed out of the ground in April, having ftood out during the winter, tho' they will not laft long after, and commonly more fticky and hard in the centre.

Carrots, are managed as it refpects plowing and rich ground, fimilarly to Parfnips. The yellow are better than the orange or red; middling fiz'd, that is, a foot long and two inches thick at the top end, are better than over grown ones ; they are cultivated beft with onions, fowed very thin, and mixed with other feeds, while young or fix weeks after fown, efpecially if with onions on true onion ground. They are good with veal cookery, rich in foups, excellent with hafh, in May and June.

Garlicks, tho' ufed by the French, are better a-dapted to the ufes of medicine than cookery.

Afparagus—The mode of cultivation belongs to gardening ; your bufinefs is only to cut and drefs, the largeft is beft, the growth of a day fufficient, fix inches long, and cut juft above the ground ; many cut below the furface, under an idea of getting tender fhoots, and preferving the bed ; but it enfeebles the root : dig round it and it will be wet with the juices— but if cut above ground, and juft as the dew is going off, the fun will either reduce the juice, or fend it back to nourifh the root—its an excellent vegetable.

Parfley, of the three kinds, the thickeft and branch-ieft is the beft, is fown among onions, or in a bed by itfelf, may be dryed for winter ufe; tho' a method which I have experienced, is much better—In September I dig my roots, procure an old thin ftave dry cafk, bore holes an inch diameter in every ftave, 6 inches afunder round the cafk, and up to the top— take firft a half bufhel of rich garden mold and put into the cafk, then run the roots through the ftaves, leaving the branches outfide, prefs the earth tight a-bout the root within, and thus continue on thro' the respective stories, till the cask is full ; it being filled, run an iron bar thro' the center of the dirt in the cask, and fill with water, let stand on the south and east side of a building till frosty night, then remove it, (by flinging a rope round the cask) into the cellar ; where, during the winter, I clip with my scissars the fresh parsley, which my neighbors or myself have occasion for ; and in the spring transplant the roots in the bed in the garden, or in any unused corner— or let stand upon the wharf, or the wash shed. Its an useful mode of cultivation, and a pleasurably tasted herb, and much used in garnishing viands.

Raddish, Salmon coloured is the best, *purple* next best—*white*—*turnip*—each are produced from southern seeds, annually. They grow thriftiest sown among onions. The turnip Raddish will last well through the winter.

Artichokes—The Jerusalem is best, are cultivated like potatoes, (tho' their stocks grow 7 feet high) and may be preserved like the turnip raddish, or pickled— they like,

Horse Raddish, once in the garden, can scarcely ever be totally eradicated ; plowing or digging them up with that view, seems at times rather to increase and spread them.

Cucumbers, are of many kinds ; the prickly is best for pickles, but generally bitter ; the white is difficult to raise and tender ; choose the bright green, smooth and proper sized.

Melons—The Water Melons is cultivated on sandy soils only, above latitude 41 1-2, if a stratum of land be dug from a well, it will bring the first year good Water Melons ; the red cored are highest flavored ; a hard rine proves them ripe.

Muskmelons, are various, the rough skinned is best to eat ; the short, round, fair skinn'd, is best for Mangoes.

Lettuce, is of various kinds ; the purple spotted

leaf is generally the tenderest, and free from bitter—
Your taste must guide your market.

Cabbage, requires a page, they are so multifarious.
Note, all Cabbages have a higher relish that grow on
new unmatured grounds ; if grown in an old town
and on old gardens, they have a rankness, which at
times, may be perceived by a fresh air traveller. This
observation has been experienced for years—that Cabbages require new ground, more than Turnips.

The Low Dutch, only will do in old gardens.

The *Early Yorkshire,* must have rich soils, they will
not answer for winter, they are easily cultivated, and
frequently bro't to market in the fall. but will not
last the winter.

The *Green Savoy,* with the richest crinkles, is fine
and tender ; and altho' they do not head like the
Dutch or Yorkshire, yet the tenderness of the out
leaves is a counterpoise, it will last thro' the winter,
and are high flavored.

The *Yellow Savoy,* takes next rank, but will not
last so long ; all Cabbages will mix, and participate
of other species, like Indian Corn ; they are cul d,
best in pl nts ; and a true gardener will, in the plant
describe those which will head, and which will not.
This is new, but a fact.

The gradations in the Savoy Cabbage are discerned
by the leaf ; the richest and most scollup'd, and crink-
led, and thickest Green Savoy, falls little short of a
Colliflour.

The red and redest small tight heads, are best for
slaw, it will not boil well, comes out black or blue,
and tinges other things with which it is boiled.

B E A N S.

The *Clabboard Bean,* is easiest cultivated and collected, are good for string beans, will shell—must be
poled.

The *Windsor Bean,* is an earlier, good string, or
shell Bean.

Crambury Bean, is rich, but not univerfally approved equal to the other two.

Froſt Bean, is good only to ſhell.

Six Weeks Bean, is a yellowiſh Bean, and early bro't forward, and tolerable.

Lazy Bean, is tough, and needs no pole.

Engliſh Bean, what *they* denominate the *Horſe Bean*, is mealy when young, is profitable, eaſily cultivated, and may be grown on worn out grounds ; as they may be raiſed by boys, I cannot but recommend the more extenſive cultivation of them.

The ſmall White Bean, is beſt for winter uſe, and excellent.

Calivanſe, are run out, a yellow ſmall buſh, a black ſpeck or eye, are tough and taſteleſs, and little worth in cookery, and ſcarcely bear exportation.

Peas—Green Peas.

The Crown Imperial, takes rank in point of flavor, they bloſſom, purple and white on the top of the vines, will run from three to five feet high, ſhould be ſet in light ſandy ſoil only, or they run too much to vines.

The Crown Pea, is ſecond in richneſs of flavor.

The Rondeheval, is large and bitteriſh.

Early Carlton, is produced firſt in the ſeaſon—good.

Marrow Fats, green, yellow, and is large, eaſily cultivated, not equal to others.

Sugar Pea, needs no buſh, the pods are tender and good to eat, eaſily cultivated.

Spaniſh Manratto, is a rich Pea, requires a ſtrong high buſh.

All Peas ſhould be picked *carefully* from the vines as ſoon as dew is off, ſhelled and cleaned without water, and boiled immediately ; they are thus the richeſt flavored.

Herbs, uſeful in Cookery.

Thyme, is good in ſoups and ſtuffings.

Sweet Marjoram, is uſed in Turkeys.

Summer Savory, ditto, and in Saufages and falted Beef, and legs of Pork.

Sage, is ufed in Cheefe and Pork, but not generally approved.

Parfley, good in *foups*, and to *garnifh roaft Beef*, excellent with bread and butter in the fpring.

Penny Royal, is a high aromatic, altho' a fpontaneous herb in old ploughed fields, yet might be more generally cultivated in gardens, and ufed in cookery and medicines.

Sweet Thyme, is moft ufeful and beft approved in cookery.

F R U I T S.

Pears, There are many different kinds ; but the large Bell Pear, fometimes called the Pound Pear, the yelloweft is the beft, and in the fame town they differ effentially.

Hard Winter Pear, are innumerable in their qualities, are good in fauces, and baked.

Harveft and *Summer Pear* are a tolerable defert, are much improved in this country, as all other fruits are by grafting and innoculation.

Apples, are ftill more various, yet rigidly retain their own fpecies, and are highly ufeful in families, and ought to be more univerfally cultivated, excepting in the compacteft cities. There is not a fingle family but might fet a tree in fome otherwife ufelefs fpot, which might ferve the two fold ufe of fhade and fruit ; on which 12 or 14 kinds of fruit trees might eafily be engrafted, and effentiallypreferve the orchard from the intrufions of boys, &c. which is too common in America. If the boy who thus planted a tree, and guarded and protected it in a ufelefs corner, and carefully engrafted different fruits, was to be indulged free accefs into orchards, whilft the neglectful boy was prohibited—how many millions of fruit trees would fpring into growth—and what a faving to the union. The net faving would in time extinguifh the public debt, and enrich our cookery.

Currants, are eafily grown from fhoots trimmed off from old bunches,and fet carelefsly in the ground; they flourifh on all foils, and make good jellies— their cultivation ought to be encouraged.

Black Currants, may be cultivated—but until they can be dryed, and until fugars are propagated, they are in a degree unprofitable.

Grapes, are natural to the climate; grow fpontaneoufly in every ftate in the union, and ten degrees north of the line of the union, The *Madeira, Lifbon* and *Malaga* Grapes, are cultivated in gardens in this country, and are a rich treat or defert. Trifling attention only is neceffary for their ample growth.

Having pointed out the *beft methods of judging of the qualities of Viands, Poultry, Fifh, Vegetables, &c.* We now prefent the beft approved methods of DRESSING and COOKING them; and to fuit all taftes, prefent the following

RECEIPTS.

To Roaft Beef.

THE general rules are, to have a brifk hot fire, to hang down rather than to fpit, to bafte with falt and water, and one quarter of an hour to every pound of beef, tho' tender beef will require lefs, while old tough beef will require more roafting; pricking with a fork will determine you whether done or not; rare done is the healthieft and the tafte of this age.

Roaft Mutton.

If a breaft let it be cauled, if a leg, ftuffed or not, let it be done more gently than beef, and done more; the chine, faddle or leg require more fire and longer time than the breaft, &c. Garnifh with fcraped horfe radifh, and ferve with potatoes, beans, colliflowers, water-creffes, or boiled onion, caper fauce, mafhed turnip, or lettuce.

Roaſt Veal.

As it is more tender than beef or mutton, and eaſily ſcorched, paper it, eſpecially the fat parts, lay it ſome diſtance from the fire a while to heat gently, baſte it well ; a 15 pound piece requires one hour and a quarter roaſting; garniſh with green-parſley and ſliced lemon.

Roaſt Lamb.

Lay down to a clear good fire that will not want ſtirring or altering, baſte with butter, duſt on flour, baſte with the dripping, and before you take it up, add more butter and ſprinkle on a little ſalt and parſly ſhred fine ; ſend to table with a nice ſallad, green peas, freſh beans, or a colliflower, or aſparagus.

To ſtuff a Turkey.

Grate a wheat loaf, one quarter of a pound butter, one quarter of a pound ſalt pork, finely chopped, 2 eggs, a little ſweet marjoram, ſummer ſavory, parſley and ſage, pepper and ſalt (if the pork be not ſufficient,) fill the bird and ſew up.

The ſame will anſwer for all Wild Fowl.

Water Fowls require onions.

The ſame ingredients ſtuff a *leg of Veal, freſh Pork* or a *loin of Veal.*

To ſtuff and roaſt a Turkey, or Fowl.

One pound ſoft wheat bread, 3 ounces beef ſuet, 3 eggs, a little ſweet thyme, ſweet marjoram, pepper and ſalt, and ſome add a gill of wine ; fill the bird therewith and ſew up, hang down to a ſteady ſolid fire, baſting frequently with ſalt and water, and roaſt until a ſteam emits from the breaſt, put one third of a pound of butter into the gravy, duſt flour over the bird and baſte with the gravy ; ſerve up with boiled onions and cramberry-ſauce, mangoes, pickles or celery.

2. Others omit the ſweet herbs, and add parſley done with potatoes.

3. Boil and maſh 3 pints potatoes, wet them with butter, add ſweet herbs, pepper, ſalt, fill and roaſt as above.

To ftuff and roaft a Goflin.

Boil the inwards tender, chop them fine, put double quantity of grated bread, 4 ounces butter, pepper, falt, (and fweet herbs if you like) 2 eggs moulded into the ftuffing, parboil 4 onions and chop them into the ftuffing, add wine, and roaft the bird.

The above is a good ftuffing for every kind of Water Fowl, which requires onion fauce.

To fmother a Fowl in Oyfters.

Fill the bird with dry Oyfters, and few up and boil in water juft fufficient to cover the bird, falt and feafon to your tafte—when done tender, put into a deep difh and pour over it a pint of ftewed oyfters, well buttered and peppered, garnifh a turkey with fprigs of parfley or leaves of cellery : a fowl is beft with a parfley fauce.

To ftuff a Leg of Veal.

Take one pound of veal, half pound pork (falted,) one pound grated bread, chop all very fine, with a handful of green parfley, pepper it, add 3 ounces butter and 3 eggs, (and fweet herbs if you like them,) cut the leg round like a ham and ftab it full of holes, and fill in all the ftuffing ; then falt and pepper the leg and duft on fome flour ; if baked in an oven, put into a fauce pan with a little water, if potted, lay fome fcewers at the bottom of the pot, put in a little water and lay the leg on the fcewers, with a gentle fire render it tender, (frequently adding water,) when done take out the leg, put butter in the pot and brown the leg, the gravy in a feparate veffel muft be thickened and buttered and a fpoonful of ketchup added.

To ftuff a leg of Pork to bake or roaft.

Corn the leg 48 hours and ftuff with faufage meat and bake in a hot oven two hours and an half or roaft.

To alamode a round of Beef.

To a 14 or 16 pound round of beef, put one ounce falt-petre, 48 hours after ftuff it with the fol-.

lowing : one and half pound beef, one pound falt
pork, two pound grated bread, chop all fine and rub
in half pound butter, falt, pepper and cayenne, fum-
mer favory, thyme ; lay it on fcewers in a large pot,
over 3 pints hot water (which it muft occafionally
be fupplied with,) the fteam of which in 4 or 5 hours
will render the round tender if over a moderate fire;
when tender, take away the gravy and thicken with
flour and butter, and boil, brown the round with butter and flour, adding ketchup and wine to your tafte.

To alamode a round.

Take fat pork cut in flices or mince, feafon it with
pepper, falt, fweet marjoram and thyme, cloves,
mace and nutmeg, make holes in the beef and ftuff
it the night before cooked ; put fome bones acrofs
the bottom of the pot to keep from burning, put in
one quart Claret wine, one quart water and one onion ; lay the round on the bones, cover clofe and
ftop it round the top with dough ; hang on in the
morning and ftew gently two hours ; turn it, and
ftop tight and ftew two hours more ; when done tender, grate a cruft of bread on the top and brown it
before the fire ; fcum the gravy and ferve in a butter
boat, ferve it with the refidue of the gravy in the
difh.

To Drefs a Turtle.

Fill a boiler or kettle, with a quantity of water fufficient to fcald the callapach and Callapee, the fins, &c.
and about 9 o'clock hang up your Turtle by the
hind fins, cut of the head and fave the blood, take a
fharp pointed knife and feparate the callapach from
the callapee, or the back from the belly part, down
to the fhoulders, fo as to come at the entrails which
take out, and clean them, as you would thofe of any
other animal, and throw them into a tub of clean water, taking great care not to break the gall, but to
cut it off from the liver and throw it away, then feparate each diftinctly and put the guts into another
veffel, open them with a fmall pen-knife end to end,

wafh them clean, and draw them through a woolen cloth, in warm water, to clear away the flime and then put them in clean cold water till they are ufed with the other part of the entrails, which mult be cut up fmall to be mixed in the baking difhes with the meat ; this done, feparate the back and belly pieces, entirely cutting away the fore fins by the upper joint, which fcald; peal off the loofe fkin and cut them into fmall pieces, laying them by themfelves, either in another veffel, or on the table, ready to be feafoned ; then cut off the meat from the belly part, and clean the back from the lungs, kidneys, &c. and that meat cut into pieces as fmall as a walnut, laying it likewife by itfelf; after this you are to fcald the back, and belly pieces, pulling off the fhell from the back, and the yellow fkin from the belly, when all will be white and clean, and with the kitchen cleaver cut thofe up likewife into pieces about the bignefs or breadth of a card ; put thofe pieces into clean cold water, wafh them and place them in a heap on the table, fo that each part may lay by itfelf; the meat being thus prepared and laid feparate for feafoning ; mix two third parts of falt or rather more, and one third part of cyanne pepper, black pepper, and a nutmeg, and mace pounded fine, and mixt all together ; the quantity, to be proportioned to the fize of the Turtle, fo that in each difh there may be about three fpoonfuls of feafoning to every twelve pound of meat ; your meat being thus feafoned, get fome fweet herbs, fuch as thyme, favory, &c. let them be dryed and rub'd fine, and having provided fome deep difhes to bake it in, which fhould be of the common brown ware, put in the coarfeft part of the meat, put a quarter pound of butter at the bottom of each difh, and then put fome of each of the feveral parcels of meat, fo that the difhes may be all alike and have equal portions of the different parts of the Turtle, and between each laying of meat ftrew a little of the mixture of fweet herbs, fill your difhes within an inch an half, or two inches of the top ; boil the blood of the Turtle, and put into it, then lay on forcemeat balls made of veal, highly feafoned with the fame feafoning as the Turtle; put in each difh a gill of Madeira Wine, and as much water as it will conveniently hold, then break over it five or fix eggs to keep the meat from fcorching at the top, and over that fhake a handful of fhread parfley, to make it look green, when done put your difhes into an oven made hot enough to bake bread, and in an hour and half, or two hours (according to the fize of the difhes) it will be fufficiently done.

To drefs a Calve's Head. Turtle fafhion.

The head and feet being well fcalded and cleaned, open the head, taking the brains, wafh, pick and cleanfe, falt and pepper and parfley them and put bye in a cloth; boil the head, feet and heartflet one and quarter, or one and half hour, fever out the bones, cut the fkin and meat in flices, ftrain the liquor in which boiled and put by; clean the pot very clean or it will burn too, make a layer of the flices, which duft with a compofition made of black pepper one fpoon, of fweet herbs pulverized, two fpoons (fweet marjoram and thyme are moft approved) a tea fpoon of cayenne, one pound butter, then duft with flour, then a layer of flices with flices of veal and feafoning till compleated, cover with the liquor, ftew gently three quarters of an hour. To make the forced meat balls—take one and half pound veal, one pound grated bread, 4 ounces raw falt pork, mince and feafon with above and work with 3 whites into balls, one or one an half inch diameter, roll in flour, and fry in very hot butter till brown, then chop the brains fine and ftir into the whole mefs in the pot, put thereto, one third part of the fryed balls and a pint wine or lefs, when all is heated thro' take off and ferve in tureens, laying the refidue of the balls and hard boiled and pealed eggs into a difh, garnifh with flices of lemon.

A Stew Pie.

Boil a fhoulder of Veal, and cut up, falt, pepper,

and butter half pound, and flices of raw falt pork, make a layer of meat, and a layer of bifcuit, or bifcuit dough into a pot, cover clofe and ftew half an hour in three quarts of water only.

A *Sea Pie*.

Four pound of flour, one and half pound of butter rolled into pafte, wet with cold water, line the pot therewith, lay in fplit pigeons, turkey pies, veal, mutton or birds, with flices of pork, falt, pepper, and duft on flour, doing thus till the pot is full or your ingredients expended, add three pints water, cover tight with pafte, and ftew moderately two and half hours.

A *Chicken Pie*.

Pick and clean fix chickens, (without fcalding) take out their inwards and wafh the birds while whole, then joint the birds, falt and pepper the pieces and inwards. Roll one inch thick pafte No. 8 and cover a deep difh, and double at the rim or edge of the difh, put thereto a layer of chickens and a layer of thin flices of butter, till the chickens and one and a half pound butter are expended, which cover with a thick pafte; bake one and a half hour.

Or if your oven be poor, parboil the chickens with half a pound of butter, and put the pieces with the remaining one pound of butter, and half the gravy into the pafte, and while boiling, thicken the refidue of the gravy, and when the pie is drawn, open the cruft, and add the gravy.

Minced Pies. A Foot Pie.

Scald neets feet, and clean well, (grafs fed are beft) put them into a large veffel of cold water, which change daily during a week, then boil the feet till tender, and take away the bones, when cold, chop fine, to every four pound minced meat, add one pound of beef fuet, and four pound apple raw, and a little falt, chop all together very fine, add one quart of wine, two pound of ftoned raifins, one ounce of cinnamon, one ounce mace, and fweeten to your tafte; make ufe of pafte No. 3—bake three quarters of an hour.

Weeks after, when you have occasion to use them, carefully raise the top crust, and with a round edg'd spoon, collect the meat into a bason, which warm with additional wine and spices to the taste of your circle, while the crust is also warm'd like a hoe cake, put carefully together and serve up, by this means you can have hot pies through the winter, and enrich'd singly to your company.

Tongue Pie.

One pound neat's tongue, one pound apple, one third of a pound of Sugar, one quarter of a pound of butter, one pint of wine, one pound of raisins, or currants, (or half of each) half ounce of cinnamon and mace—bake in paste No. 1, in proportion to size.

Minced Pie of Beef.

Four pound boild beef, chopped fine, and salted; six pound of raw apple chopped also, one pound beef suet, one quart of Wine or rich sweet cyder, one ounce mace, and cinnamon, a nutmeg, two pounds raisins, bake in paste No. 3, three fourths ofan hour.

Observations.

All meat pies require a hotter and brisker oven than fruit pies, in good cookeries, all raisins should be stoned.—As people differ in their tastes, they may alter to their wishes. And as it is difficult to ascertain with precision the small articles of spicery; every one may relish as they like, and suit their taste.

Apple Pie.

Stew and strain the apples, to every three pints, grate the peal of a fresh lemon, add cinnamon, mace, rose-water and sugar to your taste—and bake in paste No. 3.

Every species of fruit such as peas, plums, rasberries, black berries may be only sweetned, without spices—and bake in paste No. 3.

Currant Pies.

Take green, full grown currants, and one third their quantity of sugar, proceeding as above.

A buttered apple Pie.

Pare, quarter and core tart apples, lay in paſte
No. 3, cover with the ſame ; bake half an hour,
when drawn, gently raiſe the top cruſt, add ſugar
butter, cinnamon, mace, wine or roſe-water q : ſ:

PUDDINGS.
A Rice Pudding.

One quarter of a pound rice, a ſtick of cinnamon,
to a quart of milk (ſtirred often to keep from
burning) and boil quick, cool and add half a nutmeg,
4 ſpoons roſe-water, 8 eggs ; butter or puff paſte a
diſh and pour the above compoſition into it, and
bake one and half hour.

No. 2. Boil 6 ounces rice in a quart milk, on a ſlow
fire 'till tender, ſtir in one pound butter, interim
beet 14 eggs, add to the pudding when cold with ſugar, ſalt, roſe-water and ſpices to your taſte, adding
raiſins or currants, bake as No. 1.

No. 3. 8 ſpoons rice boiled in 2 quarts milk,
when cooled add 8 eggs, 6 ounces butter, wine, ſugar and ſpices, q: ſ: bake 2 hours.

No. 4. Boil in water half pound ground rice till
ſoft, add 2 quarts milk and ſcald, cool and add 8
eggs, 6 ounces butter, 1 pound raiſins, ſalt, cinnamon and a ſmall nutmeg, bake 2 hours.

No. 5. *A cheap one*, half pint rice, 2 quarts milk,
ſalt, butter, allſpice, put cold into a hot oven, bake
2 and half hours.

No. 6. Put 6 ounces rice into water, or milk and
water, let it ſwell or ſoak tender, then boil gently,
ſtirring in a little butter, when cool ſtir in a quart
cream, 6 or 8 eggs well beaten, and add cinnamon
nutmeg, and ſugar to your taſte, bake.

N. B. The mode of introducing the ingredients,
is a material point ; in all caſes where eggs are mentioned it is underſtood to be well beat ; whites and
yolks and the ſpices, fine and ſettled.

A Nice Indian Pudding.

No. 1. 3 pints fcalded milk, 7 fpoons fine Indian meal, ftir well together while hot, let ftand till cooled; add 7 eggs, half pound raifins, 4 ounces butter, fpice and fugar, bake one and half hour.

No. 2. 3 pints fcalded milk to one pint meal falted; cool, add 2 eggs, 4 ounces butter, fugar or molaffes and fpice q. f. it will require two and half hours baking.

No. 3. Salt a pint meal, wet with one quart milk, fweeten and put into a ftrong cloth, brafs or bell metal veffel, ftone or earthern pot, fecure from wet and boil 12 hours.

A Sunderland Pudding.

Whip 6 eggs, half the whites, take half a nutmeg, one point cream and a little falt, 4 fpoons fine flour, oil or butter pans, cups, or bowls, bake in a quick oven one hour. Eat with fweet fauce.

A Whitpot.

Cut half a loaf of bread in flices, pour thereon 2 quarts milk, 6 eggs, rofe-water, nutmeg and half pound of fugar; put into a difh and cover with pafte, No. 1. bake flow 1 hour.

A Bread Pudding.

One pound foft bread or bifcuit foaked in one quart milk, run thro' a fieve or cullender, add 7 eggs, three quarters of a pound fugar, one quarter of a pound butter, nutmeg or cinnamon, one gill rofe-water, one pound ftoned raifins, half pint cream, bake three quarters of an hour, middling oven.

A Flour Pudding.

Seven eggs, one quarter of a pound of fugar, and a tea fpoon of falt, beat and put to one quart milk, 5 fpoons of flour, cinnamon and nutmeg to your tafte, bake half an hour, and ferve up with fweet fauce.

A boiled Flour Pudding.

One quart milk, 9 eggs, 7 fpoons flour, a little falt, put into a ftrong cloth and boiled three quarters of an hour.

A Cream Almond Pudding.

Boil gently a little mace and half a nutmeg (grated) in a quart cream ; when cool, beat 8 yolks and 3 whites, ftrain and mix with one fpoon flour one quarter of a pound almonds ; fettled, add one fpoon rofe-water, and by degrees the cold cream and beat well together ; wet a thick cloth and flour it, and pour in the pudding, boil hard half an hour, take out, pour over it melted butter and fugar.

An apple Pudding Dumplin.

Put into pafte, quartered apples, lye in a cloth and boil two hours, ferve with fweet fauce.

Pears, Plumbs, &c,

Are done the fame way.

Potatoe Pudding. Baked.

No. 1. One pound boiled potatoes, one pound fugar, half a pound butter, 10 eggs.

No. 2. One pound boiled potatoes, mafhed, three quarters of a pound butter, 3 gills milk or cream, the juice of one lemon and the peal grated, half a pound fugar, half nutmeg, 7 eggs (taking out 3 whites,) 2 fpoons rofe-water.

Apple Pudding.

One pound apple fifted, one pound fugar, 9 eggs, one quarter of a pound butter, one quart fweet cream, one gill rofe-water, a cinnamon, a green lemon peal grated (if fweet apples,) add the juice of half a lemon, put on to pafte No. 7. Currants, raifins and citron fome add, but good without them.

Carrot Pudding.

A coffee cup full of boiled and ftrained carrots, 5 eggs, 2 ounces fugar and butter each, cinnamon and rofe water to your tafte, baked in a deep difh without pafte.

A Crookneck, or Winter Squafh Pudding.

Core, boil and fkin a good fquafh, and bruize it well ; take 6 large apples, pared, cored, and ftewed tender, mix together ; add 6 or 7 fpoonsful of dry bread or bifcuit, rendered fine as meal, half pint milk

or cream, 2 fpoons of rofe-water, 2 do. wine, 5 or 6
eggs beaten and ftrained, nutmeg, falt and fugar to
your tafte, one fpoon flour, beat all fmartly together,
bake.

The above is a good receipt for Pompkins, Potatoes or Yams, adding more moiftening or milk and
rofe water, and to the two latter a few black or Lifbon currants, or dry whortleberries fcattered in, will
make it better.

Pompkin.

No. 1.   One quart ftewed and ftrained, 3 pints
cream, 9 beaten eggs, fugar, mace, nutmeg and ginger, laid into pafte No. 7 or 3, and with a dough
fpur, crofs and chequer it, and baked in difhes three
quarters of an hour.

No. 2.   One quart of milk, 1 pint pompkin, 4
eggs, molaffes, allfpice and ginger in a cruft, bake
1 hour.

Orange Pudding.

Put fixteen yolks with half a pound butter melted,
grate in the rinds of two Seville oranges, beat in
half pound of fine Sugar, add two fpoons orange water, two of rofe-water, one gill of wine, half pint
cream, two naples bifcuit or the crumbs of a fine
loaf, or roll foaked in cream, mix all together, put
it into rich puff-pafte, which let be double round the
edges of the difh ; bake like a cuftard.

A Lemon Pudding.

1. Grate the yellow of the peals of three lemons,
then take two whole lemons, roll under your hand
on the table till foft, taking care not to burft them,
cut and fqueeze them into the grated peals.

2. Take ten ounces foft wheat bread, and put a
pint of fcalded white wine thereto, let foak and put
to No. 1.

3. Beat four whites and eight yolks, and put to
above, adding three quarters of a pound of melted
butter, (which let be very frefh and good) one pound
fine fugar, beat all together till thorougly mixed.

4. Lay paſte No. 7 or 9 on a diſh, plate or ſaucers, and fill with above compoſition.

5. Bake near 1 hour, and when baked—ſtick on pieces of paſte, cut with a jagging iron or a dough-ſpur to your fancy, baked lightly on a floured paper; garniſhed thus, they may be ſerved hot or cold.

Puff Paſtes for Tarts.

No. 1. Rub one pound of butter into one pound of flour, whip 2 whites and add with cold water and one yolk; make into paſte, roll in in ſix or ſeven times one pound of butter, flowring it each roll. This is good for any ſmall thing.

No. 2. Rub ſix pound of butter into fourteen pound of flour, eight eggs, add cold water, make a ſtiff paſte.

No. 3. To any quantity of flour, rub in three fourths of it's weight of butter, (twelve eggs to a peck) rub in one third or half, and roll in the reſt.

No. 4. Into two quarts flour (ſalted) and wet ſtiff with cold water roll in, in nine or ten times one and half pound of butter.

No. 5. One pound flour, three fourths of a pound of butter, beat well.

No. 6. To one pound of flour rub in one fourth of a pound of butter wet with three eggs and rolled in a half pound of butter.

A Paſte for Sweet Meats.

No. 7. Rub one third of one pound of butter, and one pound of lard into two pound of flour, wet with four whites well beaten; water q : ſ : to make a paſte, roll in the reſidue of ſhortning in ten or twelve roll-ings—bake quick.

No. 8. Rub in one and half pound of ſuet to ſix pounds of flour, and a ſpoon full of ſalt, wet with cream roll in, in ſix or eight times, two and half pounds of butter—good for a chicken or meat pie.

Royal Paſte,

No. 9. Rub half a pound of butter into one pound of flour, four whites beat to a foam, add two yolks,

two ounces of fine fugar; roll often, rubbing one
third, and rolling two thirds of the butter is beft;
excellent for tarts and apple cakes.

CUSTARDS.

1. One pint cream fweetened to your tafte, warmed
hot ; ftir in fweet wine, till curdled, grate in cinnamon
and nutmeg.

2. Sweeten a quart of milk, add nutmeg, wine,
brandy, rofe-water and fix eggs ; bake in tea cups or
difhes, or boil in water, taking care that it don't boil
into the cups.

3. Put a ftick of cinnamon to one quart of milk,
boil well, add fix eggs, two fpoons of rofe-water—
bake.

4. *Boiled Cuſtard*—one pint of cream, two ounces
of almonds, two fpoons of rofe-water, or orange flower water, fome mace ; boil thick, then ftir in fweet-
ning, and lade off into china cups, and ferve up.

Rice Cuſtard.

Boil a little mace, a quartered nutmeg in a quart
of cream, add rice (well boiled) while boiling
fweeten and flavor with orange or rofe water, putting
into cups or difhes , when cooled, fet to ferve up.

A Rich Cuſtard.

Four eggs beat and put to one quart cream, fweetened to your tafte, half a nutmeg, and a little cinnamon—baked.

A ſick bed Cuſtard.

Scald a quart milk, fweeten and falt a little, whip
3 eggs and ftir in, bake on coals in a pewter veffel.

TARTS.
Apple Tarts.

Stew and ftrain the apples, add cinnamon, rofe-
water, wine and fugar to your tafte, lay in pafte, royal, fqueeze thereon orange juice—bake gently.

Cramberries.

Stewed, ftrained and fweetened, put into pafte No.
9, and baked gently.

Marmalade, laid into pafte No. 1, baked gently.

Appricots, muft be neither pared, cut or ftoned, but put in whole, and fugar fifted over them, as above.

Orange or Lemon Tart.

Take 6 large lemons, rub them well in falt, put them into falt and water and let reft 2 days, change them daily in frefh water, 14 days, then cut flices and mince as fine as you can and boil them 2 or 3 hours till tender, then take 6 pippins, pare, quarter and core them, boil in 1 pint fair water till the pippins break, then put the half of the pippins, with all the liquor to the orange or lemon, and add one pound fugar, boil all together one quarter of an hour, put into a gallipot and fqueeze thereto a frefh orange, one fpoon of which, with a fpoon of the pulp of the pippin, laid into a thin royal pafte, laid into fmall fhallow pans or faucers, brufhed with melted butter, and fome fuperfine fugar fifted thereon, with a gentle baking, will be very good.

N. B. paftry pans, or faucers, muft be buttered lightly before the pafte is laid on. If glafs or China be ufed, have only a top cruft, you can garnifh with cut pafte, like a lemon pudding or ferve on pafte No. 7.

Goofeberry Tart.

Lay clean berries and fift over them fugar, then berries and fugar 'till a deep difh be filled, cover with pafte No. 9, and bake fome what more than other tarts.

Grapes, muft be cut in two and ftoned and done like a Goofeberry.

SYLLABUBS.

To make a fine Syllabub from the Cow.

Sweeten a quart of cyder with double refined fugar, grate nutmeg into it, then milk your cow into your liquor, when you have thus added what quantity of milk you think proper, pour half a pint or more, in proportion to the quantity of fyllabub you make, of the fweeteft cream you can get all over it.

A *Whipt Syllabub.*

Take two porringers of cream and one of white wine, grate in the ſkin of a lemon, take the whites of three eggs, ſweeten it to your taſte, then whip it with a whiſk, take off the froth as it riſes and put it into your ſyllabub glaſſes or pots , and they are fit for uſe.

To make a fine Cream.

Take a pint of cream, ſweeten it to your pallate, grate a little nutmeg, put in a ſpoonful of orange flower water and roſe water, and two ſponfuls of wine; beat up four eggs and two whites, ſtir it all together one way over the fire till it is thick, have cups ready and pour it in.

Lemon Cream.

Take the juice of four large lemons, half a pint of water, a pound of double refined ſugar beaten fine, the whites of ſeven eggs and the yolk of one beaten very well; mix altogether, ſtrain it, ſet it on a gentle fire, ſtiring it all the while and ſkim it clean, put into it the peal of one lemon, when it is very hot, but not to boil; take out the lemon peal and pour it into china diſhes.

Raſpberry Cream.

Take a quart of thick ſweet cream and boil it two or three wallops, then take it off the fire and ſtrain ſome juices of raſpberries into it to your taſte, ſtir it a good while before you put your juice in, that it may be almoſt cold, when you put it to it, and afterwards ſtir it one way for almoſt a quarter of an hour; then ſweeten it to your taſte and when it is cold you may ſend it up.

Whipt. Cream.

Take a quart of cream and the whites of 8 eggs beaten with half a pint of wine; mix it together and ſweeten it to your taſte with double refined ſugar, you may perfume it (if you pleaſe) with muſk or Amber gum tied in a rag and ſteeped a little in the cream, whip it up with a whiſk and a bit of lemon peel tyed in the middle of the whifk, take off the froth with a fpoon, and put into glaffes.

A Trifle.

Fill a difh with bifcuit finely broken, rufk and fpiced cake, wet with wine, then pour a good boil'd cuftard, (not too thick) over the rufk, and put a fyllabub over that; garnifh with jelley and flowers.

C A K E.

Plumb Cake.

Mix one pound currants, one drachm nutmeg, mace and cinnamon each, a little falt, one pound of citron, orange peal candied, and almonds bleach'd, 6 pound of flour, (well dry'd) beat 21 eggs, and add with 1 quart new ale yeaft, half pint of wine, 3 half pints of cream and raifins, q : f:

Plain Cake.

Nine pound of flour, 3 pound of fugar, 3 pound of butter, 1 quart emptins, 1 quart milk, 9 eggs, 1 ounce of fpice, 1 gill of rofe-water, 1 gill of wine.

Another.

Three quarters of a pound of fugar, 1 pound of butter, and 6 eggs work'd into 1 pound of flour.

A rich Cake.

Rub 2 pound of butter into 5 pound of flour, add 15 eggs (not much beaten) 1 pint of emptins, 1 pint of wine, kneed up ftiff like bifcuit, cover well and put by and let rife over night.

To 2 and a half pound raifins, add 1 gill brandy, to foak over night, or if new half an hour in the morning, add them with 1 gill rofe-water and 2 and half pound of loaf fugar, 1 ounce cinnamon, work well and bake as loaf cake, No. 1.

Potatoe Cake.

Boil potatoes, peal and pound them, add yolks of eggs, wine and melted butter work with flour into pafte, fhape as you pleafe, bake and pour over them melted butter, wine and fugar.

34

Johny Cake, or Hoe Cake.

Scald 1 pint of milk and put to 3 pints of indian meal, and half pint of flower—bake before the fire. Or scald with milk two thirds of the indian meal, or wet two thirds with boiling water, add salt, molasses and shortening, work up with cold water pretty stiff, and bake as above.

Indian Slapjack.

One quart of milk, 1 pint of indian meal, 4 eggs, 4 spoons of flour, little salt, beat together, baked on gridles, or fry in a dry pan, or baked in a pan which has been rub'd with suet, lard or butter.

Loaf Cakes.

No. 1. Rub 6 pound of sugar, 2 pound of lard, 3 pound of butter into 12 pound of flour, add 18 eggs, 1 quart of milk, 2 ounces of cinnamon, 2 small nutmegs, a tea cup of coriander seed, each pounded fine and sifted, add one pint of brandy, half a pint of wine, 6 pound of stoned raisins, 1 pint of emptins, first having dried your flour in the oven, dry and roll the sugar fine, rub your shortning and sugar half an hour, it will render the cake much whiter and lighter, heat the oven with dry wood, for 1 and a half hours, if large pans be used, it will then require 2 hours baking, and in proportion for smaller loaves. To frost it. Whip 6 whites, during the baking, add 3 pound of sifted loaf sugar and put on thick, as it comes hot from the oven. Some return the frosted loaf into the oven, it injures and yellows it, if the frosting be put on immediately it does best without being returned into the oven.

Another.

No. 2. Rub 4 pound of sugar, 3 and a half pound of shortning, (half butter and half lard) into 9 pound of flour, 1 dozen of eggs, 2 ounces of cinnamon, 1 pint of milk, 3 spoonfuls coriander seed, 3 gills of brandy, 1 gill of wine, 3 gills of emptins, 4 pounds of raisins.

Another.

No. 3. Six pound of flour, 3 of fugar, 2 and a half pound of fhortning, (half butter, half lard) 6 eggs, 1 nutmeg, 1 ounce of cinnamon and 1 ounce of coriander feed, 1 pint of emptins, 2 gills brandy, 1 pint of milk and 3 pound of raifins.

Another.

No. 4. Five pound of flour, 2 pound of butter, 2 and a half pounds of loaf fugar, 2 and a half pounds of raifins, 15 eggs, 1 pint of wine, 1 pint of emptins, 1 ounce of cinnamon, 1 gill rofe-water, 1 gill of brandy—baked like No. 1.

Another Plain cake.

No. 5. Two quarts milk, 3 pound of fugar, 3 pound of fhortning, warmed hot, add a quart of fweet cyder, this curdle, add 18 eggs, allfpice and orange to your tafte, or fennel, carroway or coriander feeds ; put to 9 pounds of flour, 3 pints emptins, and bake well.

Cookies.

One pound fugar boiled flowly in half pint water, fcum well and cool, add two tea fpoons pearl afh diffolved in milk, then two and half pounds flour, rub in 4 ounces butter, and two large fpoons of finely powdered coriander feed, wet with above ; make roles half an inch thick and cut to the fhape you pleafe ; bake fifteen or twenty minutes in a flack oven—good three weeks.

Another Chriftmas Cookey.

To three pound flour, fprinkle a tea cup of fine powdered coriander feed, rub in one pound butter, and one and half pound fugar, diffolve three tea fpoonfuls of pearl afh in a tea cup of milk, kneed all together well, roll three quarters of an inch thick, and cut or ftamp into fhape and fize you pleafe, bake flowly fifteen or twenty minutes ; tho' hard and dry at firft, if put into an earthern pot, and dry cellar, or damp room, they will be finer, fofter and better when fix months old.

Molasses Gingerbread.

One table spoon of cinnamon, some coriander or allspice, put to four tea spoons pearl ash, dissolved in half pint water, four pound flour, one quart molasses, four ounces butter, (if in summer rub in the butter, if in winter, warm the butter and molasses and pour to the spiced flour,) knead well 'till stiff, the more the better, the lighter and whiter it will be ; bake brisk fifteen minutes ; don't scorch ; before it is put in, wash it with whites and sugar beat together.

Gingerbread Cakes, or butter and sugar Gingerbread.

No. 1. Three pounds of flour, a grated nutmeg, two ounces ginger, one pound sugar, three small spoons pearl ash dissolved in cream, one pound butter, four eggs, knead it stiff, shape it to your fancy, bake 15 minutes.

Soft Gingerbread to be baked in pans.

No. 2. Rub three pounds of sugar, two pounds of butter, into four pounds of flour, add 20 eggs, 4 ounces ginger, 4 spoons rose water, bake as No. 1.

Butter drop do.

No. 3. Rub one quarter of a pound butter, one pound sugar, sprinkled with mace, into one pound and a quarter flour, add four eggs, one glass rose water, bake as No. 1.

Gingerbread.

No. 4. Three pound sugar, half pound butter, quarter of a pound of ginger, one doz. eggs, one glass rose water, rub into three pounds flour, bake as No. 1.

A cheap seed Cake.

Rub one pound sugar, half an ounce allspice into four quarts flour, into which pour one pound butter, melted in one pint milk, nine eggs, one gill emptins, (carroway seed and currants, or raisins if you please) make into two loaves, bake one and half hour.

Queens Cake.

Whip half pound butter to a cream, add 1 pound sugar, ten eggs, one glass wine, half gill rose water, and spices to your taste, all worked into one and a quarter pound flour, put into pans, cover with paper, and bake in a quick well heat oven, 12 or 16 minutes.

Pound Cake.

One pound fugar, one pound butter, one pound flour, one pound or ten eggs, rofe water one gill, fpices to your tafte; watch it well, it will bake in a flow oven in 15 minutes.

Another (called) Pound Cake.

Work three quarters of a pound butter, one pound of good fugar, 'till very white, whip ten whites to a foam, add the yolks and beat together, add one fpoon rofe water, 2 of brandy, and put the whole to one and and a quarter of a pound flour, if yet too foft add flour and bake flowly.

Soft Cakes in little pans.

One and half pound fugar, half pound butter, rubbed into two pounds flour, add one glafs wine, one do. rofe water, 18 eggs and a nutmeg.

A light Cake to bake in fmall cups.

Half a pound fugar, half a pound butter, rubbed into two pounds flour, one glafs wine, one do rofe water, two do. emptins, a nutmeg, cinnamon and currants.

Shrewfbury Cake.

One pound butter, three quarters of a pound fugar, a little mace, four eggs mixed and beat with your hand, till very light, put the compofition to one pound flour, roll into fmall cakes—bake with a light oven.

N. B. In all cafes where fpices are named, it is fuppofed that they be pounded fine and fifted; fugar muft be dryed and rolled fine; flour, dryed in an oven; eggs well beat or whipped into a raging foam.

Diet Bread.

One pound fugar, 9 eggs, beat for an hour, add to 14 ounces flour, fpoonful rofe water, one do. cinnamon or coriander, bake quick.

R U S K.—*To make.*

No. 1. Rub in half pound fugar, half pound butter, to four pound flour, add pint milk, pint emptins; when rifen well, bake in pans ten minutes, faft.

No. 2. One pound fugar, one pound butter, fix eggs, rubbed into 5 pounds flour, one quart emptins and wet with milk, fufficient to bake, as above.

No. 3. One pound fugar, one pound butter, rubbed into 6 or 8 pounds of flour, 12 eggs, one pint emptins, wet foft with milk, and bake.

No. 4. P. C. rufk. Put fifteen eggs to 4 pounds flour and make into large bifcuit; and bake double, or one top of another.

No. 5. One pint milk, one pint emptins, to be laid over night in fpunge, in morning, melt three quarters of a pound butter, one pound fugar, in another pint of milk, add luke warm, and beat till it rife well.

No. 6 Three quarters of a pound butter, one pound fugar, 12 eggs, one quart milk, put as much flour as they will wet, a fpoon of cinnamon, gill emptins, let it ftand till very puffy or light ; roll into fmall cakes and let it ftand on oiled tins while the oven is heating, bake 15 minutes in a quick oven, then wafh the top with fugar and whites, while hot.

Bifcuit.

One pound flour, one ounce butter, one egg, wet with milk and break while oven is heating, and in the fame proportion.

Butter Bifcuit.

One pint each milk and emptins, laid into flour, in fponge; next morning add one pound butter melted, not hot, and knead into as much flower as will with another pint of warmed milk, be of a fufficient confiftance to make foft—fome melt the butter in the milk.

A Butter Drop.

Four yolks, two whites, one pound flour, a quarter of a pound butter, one pound fugar, two fpoons rofe water, a little mace, baked in tin pans.

PRESERVES.
For preferving Quinces.

Take a peck of Quinces, pare them, take out the core with a fharp knife, if you wifh to have them whole; boil parings and cores with two pound froft grapes, in 3 quarts water, boil the liquor an hour and an half, or till it is thick, ftrain it through a coarfe hair fieve, add one and a quarter pound fugar to. every pound of quince; put the fugar into the firrup, fcald and fcim it till it is clear, put the quinces into the firrup, cut up two oranges and mix with the quince, hang them over a gentle fire for five hours, then put them in a ftone pot for ufe, fet them in a dry cool place.

For preferving Quinces in Loaf Sugar.

Take a peck of Quinces, put them into a kettle of cold water, hang them over the fire, boil them till they are foft, then take them out with a fork, when cold, pair them, quarter or halve them, if you like; take their weight of loaf fugar, put into a bell-metal kettle or fauce pan, with one quart of water, fcald and fkim it till it is very clear, then put in your Quinces, let them boil in the firrup for half an hour, add oranges as before if you like, then put them in ftone pots for ufe.

For preferving Strawberries.

Take two quarts of Strawberries, fqueeze them through a cloth, add half a pint of water and two pound of fugar, put it into a fauce pan, fcald and fkim it, take two pound of Strawberries with ftems on, fet your fauce pan on a chaffing difh, put as many Strawberries into the difh as you can with the ftems up without bruizing them, let them boil for about ten minutes, then take them out gently with a fork and put them into a ftone pot for ufe; when you have done the whole turn the firrup into the pot, when hot; fet them in a cool place for ufe.

Currants and *Cherries* may be done in the fame way, by adding a little more fugar.

The American Citron.

Take the rine of a large watermelon not too ripe, cut it into small pieces, take two pound of loaf sugar, one pint of water, put it all into a kettle, let it boil gently for four hours, then put it into pots for use.

To keep White Bullace, Pears, Plumbs, or Damsons, &c. for tarts or pies.

Gather them when full grown, and just as they begin to turn, pick all the largest out, save about two thirds of the fruit, to the other third put as much water as you think will cover them, boil and skim them; when the fruit is boiled very soft, strain it through a coarse hair sieve; and to every quart of this liquor put a pound and a half of sugar, boil it, and skim it very well; then throw in your fruit, just give them a scald; take them off the fire, and when cold, put them into bottles with wide mouths, pour your sirrup over them, lay a piece of white paper over them, and cover them with oil.

To make Marmalade.

To two pounds of quinces, put three quarters of a pound of sugar and a pint of springwater; then put them over the fire, and boil them till they are tender; then take them up and bruize them; then put them into the liquor, let it boil three quarters of an hour, and then put it into your pots or saucers.

To preserve Mulberries whole.

Set some mulberries over the fire in a skillet or preserving pan; draw from them a pint of juice when it is strained; then take three pounds of sugar beaten very fine, wet the sugar with the pint of juice, boil up your sugar and skim it, put in two pounds of ripe mulberries, and let them stand in the sirrup till they are thoroughly warm, then set them on the fire, and let them boil very gently; do them but half enough, so put them by in the sirrup till next day, then boil them gently again: when the sirrup is pretty thick, and will stand in round drops when it is cold, they are done enough, so put all into a gallipot for use.

To preserve Goosberries, Damsons, or Plumbs.

Gather them when dry, full grown, and not ripe; pick them one by one, put them into glass bottles that are very clean and dry, and cork them close with new corks; then put a kettle of water on the fire, and put in the bottles with care; wet not the corks, but let the water come up to the necks; make a gentle fire till they are a little codled and turn white; do not take them up till cold, then pitch the corks all over, or wax them close and thick; then set them in a cool dry cellar.

To preserve Peaches.

Put your peaches in boiling water, just give them a scald, but don't let them boil, take them out, and put them in cold water, then dry them in a sieve, and put them in long wide mouthed bottles: to half a dozen peaches take a quarter of a pound of sugar, clarify it, pour it over your peaches, and fill the bottles with brandy, stop them close, and keep them in a close place.

To preserve Apricots.

Take your apricots and pare them, then stone what you can whole; give them a light boiling in a pint of water, or according to your quantity of fruit; then take the weight of your apricots in sugar, and take the liquor which you boil them in, and your sugar, and boil it till it comes to a sirrup, and give them a light boiling, taking of the scum as it rises; when the sirrup jellies, it is enough; then take up the apricots, and cover them with the jelly, and put cut paper over them, and lay them down when cold. Or, take you plumbs before they have stones in them, which you may know by putting a pin through them, then codle them in many waters, till they are as green as grafs; peel them and codle them again; you must take the weight of them in sugar and make a sirrup; put to your sugar a pint of water; then put them in, set them on the fire to boil slowly, till

they be clear, fkimming them often, and they will be
very green. Put them up in glaffes, and keep them
for ufe,

To preferve Cherries.

Take two pounds of cherries, one pound and a
half of fugar, half a pint of fair water, melt fome fugar in it; when it is melted, put in your other fugar
and your cherries; then boil them foftly, till all the
fugar be melted; then boil them faft, and fkim
them; take them off two or three times and fhake
them, and put them on again, and let them boil faft;
and when they are of a good colour, and the firrup
will ftand, they are boiled enough.

To preferve Rafpberries.

Chufe rafpberries that are not too ripe, and take the
weight of them in fugar, wet your fugar with a little
water, and put in your berries, and let them boil foftly; take heed of breaking them; when they are
clear, take them up, and boil the firrup till it be thick
enough, then put them in again; and when they are
cold, put them up in glaffes.

To preferve Currants.

Take the weight of the currants in fugar, pick out
the feeds; take to a pound of fugar, half a pint of water, let it melt; then put in your currants and let
them do very leifurely, fkim them, and take them up,
let the firrup boil; then put them on again; and
when they are clear, and the firrup thick enough,
take them off; and when they are cold, put them up
in glaffes.

To preferve Plumbs.

Take your plumbs before they have ftones in them,
which you may know by putting a pin through them,
then codle them in many waters till they are as
green as grafs, peel them and coddle them again;
you muft take the weight of them in fugar, a pint of
water, then put them in, fet them on the fire, to boil
flowly till they be clear, fkiming them often, and they

will be very green; put them up in glaffes and keep them for ufe.

To keep Damfons.

Take damfons when they are firft ripe, pick them off carefully, wipe them clean, put them into fnuff bottles, ftop them up tight fo that no air can get to them, nor water; put nothing into the bottles but plumbs, put the bottles into cold water, hang them over the fire, let them heat flowly, let the water boil flowly for half an hour, when the water is cold take out the bottles, fet the bottles into a cold place, they will keep twelve months if the bottles are ftopped tight, fo as no air nor water can get to them. They will not keep long after the bottles are opened; the plumbs muft be hard.

Currant Jelly.

Having ftripped the currants from the ftalks, put them in a ftone jar, ftop it clofe, fet it in a kettle of boiling water, half way the jar, let it boil half an hour, take it cut and ftrain the juice through a coarfe hair fieve, to a pint of juice put a pound of fugar, fet it over a fine quick fire in a preferving pan, or a bell-metal fkillet, keep ftiring it all the time till the fugar be melted, then fkim the fkum off as faft as it rifes. When the jelly is very clear and fine, pour it into earthern or china cups, when cold, cut white papers juft the bignefs of the top of the pot, and lay on the jelly, dip thofe papers in brandy, then cover the top of the pot and prick it full of holes, fet it in a dry place; you may put fome into glaffes for prefent ufe.

To dry Peaches.

Take the faireft and ripeft peaches, pare them in-to fair water; take their weight in double refined fugar; of one half make a very thin firrup; then put in your peaches, boiling them till they look clear, then fplit and ftone them, boil them till they are ve-ry tender, lay them a draining, take the other half of the fugar, and boil it almoft to a candy; then put in your peaches, and let them lie all night then lay them on a glafs, and fet them in a ftove, till they are dry, if they are fugared too much, wipe them with a wet cloth a little; let the firft firrup be very thin, a quart of water to a pound of fugar.

To pickle or make Mangoes of Melons.

Take green melons, as many as you pleafe, and make a brine ftrong enough to bear an egg; then pour it boiling hot on the melons, keeping them down under the brine; let them ftand five or fix days; then take them out, flit them down on one fide, take out all the feeds, fcrape them well in the infide, and wafh them clean with cold water; then take a clove of a garlick, a little ginger and nutmeg fliced, and a little whole pepper; put all thefe proportionably into the melons, filling them up with muftard-feeds; then lay them in an earthern pot with the flit upwards, and take one part of muftard and two parts of vinegar, enough to cover them, pouring it upon them fcalding hot, and keep them clofe ftopped.

To pickle Barberries.

Take of white wine vinegar and water, of each an equal quantity; to every quart of this liquor, put in half a pound of cheap fugar, then pick the worft of your barberries and put into this liquor, and the beft into glaffes; then boil your pickle with the worft of your barberries, and fkim it very clean, boil it till it looks of a fine colour, then let it ftand to be cold, before you ftrain it; then ftrain it through a cloth, wringing it to get all the colour you can from the barberries; let it ftand to cool and fettle, then pour it clear into the glaffes; in a little of the pickle, boil a little fennel; when cold, put a little bit at the top of the pot or glafs, and cover it clofe with a bladder or leather. To every half pound of fugar, put a quarter of a pound of white falt.

To pickle Cucumbers.

Let your cucumbers be fmall, frefh gathered, and free from fpots; then make a pickle of falt and water, ftrong enough to bear an egg; boil the pickle and fkim it well, and then pour it upon your cucumbers, and ftive them down for twenty four hours; then ftrain them out into a cullender, and dry them well with a cloth, and take the beft white wine vinegar, with cloves, fliced mace, nutmeg, white pepper corns, long pepper, and races of ginger, (as much as you pleafe) boil them up together, and then clap the cucumbers in, with a few vine leaves, and a little falt, and as foon as they begin to turn their colour, put them into jars, ftive them down clofe, and when cold, tie on a bladder and leather.

Alamode Beef.

Take a round of beef, and ftuff it with half pound pork, half pound of butter, the foft of half a loaf of wheat bread, boil four eggs very hard, chop them up; add fweet majoram, fage, parfley, fummerfavory, and one ounce of cloves pounded, chop them all together, with two eggs very fine, and add a jill of wine, feafon very high with falt and pepper, cut holes in your beef, to put your ftuffing in, then ftick whole cloves into the beef, then put it into a two pail pot, with fticks at the bottom, if you wifh to have the beef round when done, put it into a cloth and bind it tight with 20 or 30 yards of twine, put it into your pot with two or three quarts of water, and one jill of wine, if the round be large it will take three or four hours to bake it.

For dreffing Codfifh.

Put the fifh firft into cold water and wafh it, then hang it over the fire and foak it fix hours in fcalding water, then fhift it into clean warm water, and let it fcald for one hour, it will be much better than to boil.

To boil all kinds of Garden Stuff.

In dreffing all forts of kitchen garden herbs, take care they are clean wafhed; that there be no fmall fnails, or caterpillars between the leaves; and that all the coarfe outer leaves, and the tops that have received any injury by the weather, be taken off; next wafh them in a good deal of water, and put them into a cullender to drain, care muft likewife be taken, that your pot or fauce pan be clean, well tinned, and free from fand, or greafe.

To keep Green Peas till Chriftmas.

Take young peas, fhell them, put them in a cullender to drain, then lay a cloth four or five times double on a table, then fpread them on, dry them very well, and have your bottles ready, fill them, cover them with mutton fuet fat when it is a little foft; fill the necks almoft to the top, cork them, tie a bladder and a leather over them and fet them in a dry cool place.

To boil French Beans.

Take your beans and ftring them, cut in two and then acrofs, when you have done them all, fprinkle them over with falt, ftir them together, as foon as your water boils put them in and make them boil up quick, they will be foon done and they will look of a better green than when growing in the garden if; they are very young, only break off the ends, them break in two and drefs them in the fame manner.

To boil broad Beans.

Beans require a great deal of water and it is not beft to fhell them till juft before they are ready to go into the pot, when the water boils put them in with fome picked parfley and fome falt, make them boil up quick, when you fee them begin to fall, they are done enough, ftrain them off, garnifh the difh with boiled parfley and fend plain butter in a cup or boat.

To boil green Peas.

When your peas are fhelled and the water boils which fhould not be much more than will cover them, put them in with a few leaves of mint, as foon as they boil put in a piece of butter as big as a walnut, and ftir them about, when they are done enough, ftrain them off, and fprinkle in a little falt, fhake them till the water drains off, fend them hot to the table with melted butter in a cup or boat.

To boil Afparagus.

Firft cut the white ends off about fix inches from

the head, and fcrape them from the green part down-
ward very clean, as you fcrape them, throw them into a pan of clear water, and after a little foaking, tie
them up in fmall even bundles, when your water boils,
put them in, and boil them up quick ; but by over
boiling they will lofe their heads ; cut a flice of bread
for a toaft, and toaft it brown on both fides ; when
your afparagus is done, take it up carefully ; dip the
toaft in the afparagus water, and lay it in the bottom
of your difh ; then lay the heads of the afparagus on
it, with the white ends outwards; pour a little
melted butter over the heads ; cut an orange into
fmall pieces, and ftick them between for garnifh.

To boil Cabbage.

If your cabbage is large, cut it into quarters ; if
fmall, cut it in halves ; let your water boil, then put in
a little falt, and next your cabbage with a little more
falt upon it ; make your water boil as foon as poffible,
and when the ftalk is tender, take up your cabbage into
a cullender, or fieve, that the water may drain off,
and fend it to table as hot as you can. Savoys are
dreffed in the fame manner.

For brewing Spruce Beer.

Take four ounces of hops, let them boil half an
hour in one gallon of water, ftrain the hop water
then add fixteen gallons of warm water, two gallons
of molaffes, eight ounces of effence of fpruce, diffolved in one quart of water, put it in a clean cafk, then
fhake it well together, add half a pint of emptins,
then let it ftand and work one week, if very warm
weather lefs time will do, when it is drawn off to bottle, add one fpoonful of molaffes to every bottle.

Emptins.

Take a handful of hops and about three quarts of
water, let it boil about fifteen minutes, then make a
thickening as you do for ftarch, ftrain the liquor,
when cold put a little emptins to work them, they
will keep well cork'd in a botttle five or fix weeks.

ADVERTISEMENT.

☞ THE author of the American Cookery, not having an education sufficient to prepare the work for the press, the person that was employed by her, and entrusted with the receipts, to prepare them for publication, (with a design to impose on her, and injure the sale of the book) did omit several articles very essential in some of the receipts, and placed others in their stead, which were highly injurious to them, without her consent—which was unknown to her, till after publication ; but she has removed them as far as possible, by the following

ERRATA.

Page 25. Rice pudding, No. 2 ; for one pound butter, read half pound—for 14 eggs read 8. No. 5 ; after half pint rice, add 6 ounces sugar.

Page 26. A nice Indian pudding, No. 3 ; boil only 6 hours.—A flour pudding ; read 9 spoons of flour, put in scalding milk ; bake an hour and half.—A boiled flour pudding ; 9 spoons of flour, boil an hour and half.

Page 27. A cream almond pudding ; for 8 yolks and 3 whites, read 8 eggs ; for 1 spoon flour, read 8—boil an hour and half.

Potatoe pudding, No. 1, No. 2. add a pint flour to each.

Page 29. Puff pastes for tarts, No, 3 ; for 12 eggs read 6.

Page 33. Plain cake ; for 1 quart of emptins, read 1 pint.

Page 35. Another plain cake, No. 5 ; for 9 pounds of flour, read 18 pounds.

In all Puddings, where cream is mentioned, milk may be used.

In Pastes, the white of eggs only are to be used.

GLOSSARY

GLOSSARY

amber gum, probably *ambergris,* the wax-like secretion of the sperm
    whale, now used in perfumery, formerly in cookery

bell-metal, the metallic substance of which bells are made

bladder and leather, pieces of each substance to be tied over the
    mouths of jars and bottles to secure the contents against air

bullace, a small wild or semi-domesticated plum

calavance, (calivanse), the name for certain varieties of pulse; here,
    an early variety of bean

calipash, that part of the turtle adjoining the upper shell

calipee, that part of the turtle adjoining the lower shell

caul, an enveloping membrane

chine, a "joint" made up of part of the backbone and adjoining flesh

cob, corn cob

do., abbreviation for ditto

emptins, semiliquid prepared yeast

fair, (of water) clean; pure

frost grape, a native American species, also called "chicken grape"

frowy, froughy, stale; sour; musty

frumenty, hulled wheat cooked in milk and seasoned with spice,
    sugar, etc.

gallipot, a small earthen pot

haslet, harslet, (heartslet), edible entrails; liver, heart, etc.

jagging iron or doughspur, an instrument used for ornamenting
    pastry, in the form of a toothed wheel, set in a handle, fre-
    quently a product of the carving (scrimshaw) done on whaling
    vessels

jump in the pan, a characteristic action of eels while in the process of cooking

lade, to transfer as with a ladle or scoop

mango, a pickled green melon stuffed with various condiments

neat's foot, the foot of an ox

orange flower water, a liquid distilled from orange blossoms

orange water, a liquid distilled from oranges

pannikin, a small metal vessel

pearlash, a salt obtained from the ashes of plants

pippin, a variety of apple

q.s., (quantum sufficit) as much as suffices

race, a root

run out or depreciate, to decline in quality with each planting (particularly true of potatoes grown from seed rather than from cuttings of the tuber itself)

scum, to skim

secure from wet, to place or cover so that water does not boil over into food

send it up, to send to the table

slack, (of heat) not strong; moderate

stive, to pack tightly

syllabub, sillabub, a mixture of milk or cream with wine, cider, or other acid, usually whipped to a froth

wallop, a bubbling motion made by rapidly boiling water, hence the duration of one such motion used as a measure of time in cooking

A CATALOG OF SELECTED DOVER

BOOKS IN ALL FIELDS OF INTEREST

CONCERNING THE SPIRITUAL IN ART, Wassily Kandinsky. Pioneering work by father of abstract art. Thoughts on color theory, nature of art. Analysis of earlier masters. 12 illustrations. 80pp. of text. 5⅜ x 8½. 23411-8 Pa. $3.95

ANIMALS: 1,419 Copyright-Free Illustrations of Mammals, Birds, Fish, Insects, etc., Jim Harter (ed.). Clear wood engravings present, in extremely lifelike poses, over 1,000 species of animals. One of the most extensive pictorial sourcebooks of its kind. Captions. Index. 284pp. 9 x 12. 23766-4 Pa. $12.95

CELTIC ART: The Methods of Construction, George Bain. Simple geometric techniques for making Celtic interlacements, spirals, Kells-type initials, animals, humans, etc. Over 500 illustrations. 160pp. 9 x 12. (USO) 22923-8 Pa. $9.95

AN ATLAS OF ANATOMY FOR ARTISTS, Fritz Schider. Most thorough reference work on art anatomy in the world. Hundreds of illustrations, including selections from works by Vesalius, Leonardo, Goya, Ingres, Michelangelo, others. 593 illustrations. 192pp. 7⅛ x 10¼. 20241-0 Pa. $9.95

CELTIC HAND STROKE-BY-STROKE (Irish Half-Uncial from "The Book of Kells"): An Arthur Baker Calligraphy Manual, Arthur Baker. Complete guide to creating each letter of the alphabet in distinctive Celtic manner. Covers hand position, strokes, pens, inks, paper, more. Illustrated. 48pp. 8¼ x 11. 24336-2 Pa. $3.95

EASY ORIGAMI, John Montroll. Charming collection of 32 projects (hat, cup, pelican, piano, swan, many more) specially designed for the novice origami hobbyist. Clearly illustrated easy-to-follow instructions insure that even beginning papercrafters will achieve successful results. 48pp. 8¼ x 11. 27298-2 Pa. $2.95

THE COMPLETE BOOK OF BIRDHOUSE CONSTRUCTION FOR WOOD-WORKERS, Scott D. Campbell. Detailed instructions, illustrations, tables. Also data on bird habitat and instinct patterns. Bibliography. 3 tables. 63 illustrations in 15 figures. 48pp. 5¼ x 8½. 24407-5 Pa. $2.50

BLOOMINGDALE'S ILLUSTRATED 1886 CATALOG: Fashions, Dry Goods and Housewares, Bloomingdale Brothers. Famed merchants' extremely rare catalog depicting about 1,700 products: clothing, housewares, firearms, dry goods, jewelry, more. Invaluable for dating, identifying vintage items. Also, copyright-free graphics for artists, designers. Co-published with Henry Ford Museum & Greenfield Village. 160pp. 8¼ x 11. 25780-0 Pa. $9.95

HISTORIC COSTUME IN PICTURES, Braun & Schneider. Over 1,450 costumed figures in clearly detailed engravings—from dawn of civilization to end of 19th century. Captions. Many folk costumes. 256pp. 8⅜ x 11¾. 23150-X Pa. $12.95

STICKLEY CRAFTSMAN FURNITURE CATALOGS, Gustav Stickley and L. & J. G. Stickley. Beautiful, functional furniture in two authentic catalogs from 1910. 594 illustrations, including 277 photos, show settles, rockers, armchairs, reclining chairs, bookcases, desks, tables. 183pp. 6½ x 9¼. 23838-5 Pa. $9.95

AMERICAN LOCOMOTIVES IN HISTORIC PHOTOGRAPHS: 1858 to 1949, Ron Ziel (ed.). A rare collection of 126 meticulously detailed official photographs, called "builder portraits," of American locomotives that majestically chronicle the rise of steam locomotive power in America. Introduction. Detailed captions. xi + 129pp. 9 x 12. 27393-8 Pa. $12.95

AMERICA'S LIGHTHOUSES: An Illustrated History, Francis Ross Holland, Jr. Delightfully written, profusely illustrated fact-filled survey of over 200 American lighthouses since 1716. History, anecdotes, technological advances, more. 240pp. 8 x 10¾. 25576-X Pa. $12.95

TOWARDS A NEW ARCHITECTURE, Le Corbusier. Pioneering manifesto by founder of "International School." Technical and aesthetic theories, views of industry, economics, relation of form to function, "mass-production split" and much more. Profusely illustrated. 320pp. 6⅛ x 9¼. (USO) 25023-7 Pa. $9.95

HOW THE OTHER HALF LIVES, Jacob Riis. Famous journalistic record, exposing poverty and degradation of New York slums around 1900, by major social reformer. 100 striking and influential photographs. 233pp. 10 x 7⅞. 22012-5 Pa. $10.95

FRUIT KEY AND TWIG KEY TO TREES AND SHRUBS, William M. Harlow. One of the handiest and most widely used identification aids. Fruit key covers 120 deciduous and evergreen species; twig key 160 deciduous species. Easily used. Over 300 photographs. 126pp. 5⅜ x 8½. 20511-8 Pa. $3.95

COMMON BIRD SONGS, Dr. Donald J. Borror. Songs of 60 most common U.S. birds: robins, sparrows, cardinals, bluejays, finches, more–arranged in order of increasing complexity. Up to 9 variations of songs of each species. Cassette and manual 99911-4 $8.95

ORCHIDS AS HOUSE PLANTS, Rebecca Tyson Northen. Grow cattleyas and many other kinds of orchids–in a window, in a case, or under artificial light. 63 illustrations. 148pp. 5⅜ x 8½. 23261-1 Pa. $4.95

MONSTER MAZES, Dave Phillips. Masterful mazes at four levels of difficulty. Avoid deadly perils and evil creatures to find magical treasures. Solutions for all 32 exciting illustrated puzzles. 48pp. 8¼ x 11. 26005-4 Pa. $2.95

MOZART'S DON GIOVANNI (DOVER OPERA LIBRETTO SERIES), Wolfgang Amadeus Mozart. Introduced and translated by Ellen H. Bleiler. Standard Italian libretto, with complete English translation. Convenient and thoroughly portable–an ideal companion for reading along with a recording or the performance itself. Introduction. List of characters. Plot summary. 121pp. 5¼ x 8½. 24944-1 Pa. $2.95

TECHNICAL MANUAL AND DICTIONARY OF CLASSICAL BALLET, Gail Grant. Defines, explains, comments on steps, movements, poses and concepts. 15-page pictorial section. Basic book for student, viewer. 127pp. 5⅜ x 8½. 21843-0 Pa. $4.95

BRASS INSTRUMENTS: Their History and Development, Anthony Baines. Authoritative, updated survey of the evolution of trumpets, trombones, bugles, cornets, French horns, tubas and other brass wind instruments. Over 140 illustrations and 48 music examples. Corrected and updated by author. New preface. Bibliography. 320pp. 5⅜ x 8½. 27574-4 Pa. $9.95

HOLLYWOOD GLAMOR PORTRAITS, John Kobal (ed.). 145 photos from 1926-49. Harlow, Gable, Bogart, Bacall; 94 stars in all. Full background on photographers, technical aspects. 160pp. 8⅜ x 11¼. 23352-9 Pa. $11.95

MAX AND MORITZ, Wilhelm Busch. Great humor classic in both German and English. Also 10 other works: "Cat and Mouse," "Plisch and Plumm," etc. 216pp. 5⅜ x 8½. 20181-3 Pa. $6.95

THE RAVEN AND OTHER FAVORITE POEMS, Edgar Allan Poe. Over 40 of the author's most memorable poems: "The Bells," "Ulalume," "Israfel," "To Helen," "The Conqueror Worm," "Eldorado," "Annabel Lee," many more. Alphabetic lists of titles and first lines. 64pp. 5³⁄₁₆ x 8¼. 26685-0 Pa. $1.00

PERSONAL MEMOIRS OF U. S. GRANT, Ulysses Simpson Grant. Intelligent, deeply moving firsthand account of Civil War campaigns, considered by many the finest military memoirs ever written. Includes letters, historic photographs, maps and more. 528pp. 6⅛ x 9¼. 28587-1 Pa. $11.95

AMULETS AND SUPERSTITIONS, E. A. Wallis Budge. Comprehensive discourse on origin, powers of amulets in many ancient cultures: Arab, Persian Babylonian, Assyrian, Egyptian, Gnostic, Hebrew, Phoenician, Syriac, etc. Covers cross, swastika, crucifix, seals, rings, stones, etc. 584pp. 5⅜ x 8½. 23573-4 Pa. $12.95

RUSSIAN STORIES/PYCCKNE PACCKA3bI: A Dual-Language Book, edited by Gleb Struve. Twelve tales by such masters as Chekhov, Tolstoy, Dostoevsky, Pushkin, others. Excellent word-for-word English translations on facing pages, plus teaching and study aids, Russian/English vocabulary, biographical/critical introductions, more. 416pp. 5⅜ x 8½. 26244-8 Pa. $8.95

PHILADELPHIA THEN AND NOW: 60 Sites Photographed in the Past and Present, Kenneth Finkel and Susan Oyama. Rare photographs of City Hall, Logan Square, Independence Hall, Betsy Ross House, other landmarks juxtaposed with contemporary views. Captures changing face of historic city. Introduction. Captions. 128pp. 8¼ x 11. 25790-8 Pa. $9.95

AIA ARCHITECTURAL GUIDE TO NASSAU AND SUFFOLK COUNTIES, LONG ISLAND, The American Institute of Architects, Long Island Chapter, and the Society for the Preservation of Long Island Antiquities. Comprehensive, well-researched and generously illustrated volume brings to life over three centuries of Long Island's great architectural heritage. More than 240 photographs with authoritative, extensively detailed captions. 176pp. 8¼ x 11. 26946-9 Pa. $14.95

NORTH AMERICAN INDIAN LIFE: Customs and Traditions of 23 Tribes, Elsie Clews Parsons (ed.). 27 fictionalized essays by noted anthropologists examine religion, customs, government, additional facets of life among the Winnebago, Crow, Zuni, Eskimo, other tribes. 480pp. 6⅛ x 9¼. 27377-6 Pa. $10.95

CATALOG OF DOVER BOOKS

FRANK LLOYD WRIGHT'S HOLLYHOCK HOUSE, Donald Hoffmann. Lavishly illustrated, carefully documented study of one of Wright's most controversial residential designs. Over 120 photographs, floor plans, elevations, etc. Detailed perceptive text by noted Wright scholar. Index. 128pp. 9¼ x 10¾. 27133-1 Pa. $11.95

THE MALE AND FEMALE FIGURE IN MOTION: 60 Classic Photographic Sequences, Eadweard Muybridge. 60 true-action photographs of men and women walking, running, climbing, bending, turning, etc., reproduced from rare 19th-century masterpiece. vi + 121pp. 9 x 12. 24745-7 Pa. $10.95

1001 QUESTIONS ANSWERED ABOUT THE SEASHORE, N. J. Berrill and Jacquelyn Berrill. Queries answered about dolphins, sea snails, sponges, starfish, fishes, shore birds, many others. Covers appearance, breeding, growth, feeding, much more. 305pp. 5¼ x 8¼. 23366-9 Pa. $8.95

GUIDE TO OWL WATCHING IN NORTH AMERICA, Donald S. Heintzelman. Superb guide offers complete data and descriptions of 19 species: barn owl, screech owl, snowy owl, many more. Expert coverage of owl-watching equipment, conservation, migrations and invasions, etc. Guide to observing sites. 84 illustrations. xiii + 193pp. 5⅜ x 8½. 27344-X Pa. $8.95

MEDICINAL AND OTHER USES OF NORTH AMERICAN PLANTS: A Historical Survey with Special Reference to the Eastern Indian Tribes, Charlotte Erichsen-Brown. Chronological historical citations document 500 years of usage of plants, trees, shrubs native to eastern Canada, northeastern U.S. Also complete identifying information. 343 illustrations. 544pp. 6½ x 9¼. 25951-X Pa. $12.95

STORYBOOK MAZES, Dave Phillips. 23 stories and mazes on two-page spreads: Wizard of Oz, Treasure Island, Robin Hood, etc. Solutions. 64pp. 8¼ x 11. 23628-5 Pa. $2.95

NEGRO FOLK MUSIC, U.S.A., Harold Courlander. Noted folklorist's scholarly yet readable analysis of rich and varied musical tradition. Includes authentic versions of over 40 folk songs. Valuable bibliography and discography. xi + 324pp. 5⅜ x 8½. 27350-4 Pa. $7.95

MOVIE-STAR PORTRAITS OF THE FORTIES, John Kobal (ed.). 163 glamor, studio photos of 106 stars of the 1940s: Rita Hayworth, Ava Gardner, Marlon Brando, Clark Gable, many more. 176pp. 8⅜ x 11¼. 23546-7 Pa. $12.95

BENCHLEY LOST AND FOUND, Robert Benchley. Finest humor from early 30s, about pet peeves, child psychologists, post office and others. Mostly unavailable elsewhere. 73 illustrations by Peter Arno and others. 183pp. 5⅜ x 8½. 22410-4 Pa. $6.95

YEKL and THE IMPORTED BRIDEGROOM AND OTHER STORIES OF YIDDISH NEW YORK, Abraham Cahan. Film Hester Street based on Yekl (1896). Novel, other stories among first about Jewish immigrants on N.Y.'s East Side. 240pp. 5⅜ x 8½. 22427-9 Pa. $6.95

SELECTED POEMS, Walt Whitman. Generous sampling from *Leaves of Grass*. Twenty-four poems include "I Hear America Singing," "Song of the Open Road," "I Sing the Body Electric," "When Lilacs Last in the Dooryard Bloom'd," "O Captain! My Captain!"–all reprinted from an authoritative edition. Lists of titles and first lines. 128pp. 5¾₆ x 8¼. 26878-0 Pa. $1.00

THE BEST TALES OF HOFFMANN, E. T. A. Hoffmann. 10 of Hoffmann's most important stories: "Nutcracker and the King of Mice," "The Golden Flowerpot," etc. 458pp. 5⅜ x 8½. 21793-0 Pa. $9.95

FROM FETISH TO GOD IN ANCIENT EGYPT, E. A. Wallis Budge. Rich detailed survey of Egyptian conception of "God" and gods, magic, cult of animals, Osiris, more. Also, superb English translations of hymns and legends. 240 illustrations. 545pp. 5⅜ x 8½. 25803-3 Pa. $11.95

FRENCH STORIES/CONTES FRANÇAIS: A Dual-Language Book, Wallace Fowlie. Ten stories by French masters, Voltaire to Camus: "Micromegas" by Voltaire; "The Atheist's Mass" by Balzac; "Minuet" by de Maupassant; "The Guest" by Camus, six more. Excellent English translations on facing pages. Also French-English vocabulary list, exercises, more. 352pp. 5⅜ x 8½. 26443-2 Pa. $8.95

CHICAGO AT THE TURN OF THE CENTURY IN PHOTOGRAPHS: 122 Historic Views from the Collections of the Chicago Historical Society, Larry A. Viskochil. Rare large-format prints offer detailed views of City Hall, State Street, the Loop, Hull House, Union Station, many other landmarks, circa 1904-1913. Introduction. Captions. Maps. 144pp. 9⅜ x 12¼. 24656-6 Pa. $12.95

OLD BROOKLYN IN EARLY PHOTOGRAPHS, 1865-1929, William Lee Younger. Luna Park, Gravesend race track, construction of Grand Army Plaza, moving of Hotel Brighton, etc. 157 previously unpublished photographs. 165pp. 8⅞ x 11¾. 23587-4 Pa. $13.95

THE MYTHS OF THE NORTH AMERICAN INDIANS, Lewis Spence. Rich anthology of the myths and legends of the Algonquins, Iroquois, Pawnees and Sioux, prefaced by an extensive historical and ethnological commentary. 36 illustrations. 480pp. 5⅜ x 8½. 25967-6 Pa. $8.95

AN ENCYCLOPEDIA OF BATTLES: Accounts of Over 1,560 Battles from 1479 B.C. to the Present, David Eggenberger. Essential details of every major battle in recorded history from the first battle of Megiddo in 1479 B.C. to Grenada in 1984. List of Battle Maps. New Appendix covering the years 1967-1984. Index. 99 illustrations. 544pp. 6½ x 9¼. 24913-1 Pa. $14.95

SAILING ALONE AROUND THE WORLD, Captain Joshua Slocum. First man to sail around the world, alone, in small boat. One of great feats of seamanship told in delightful manner. 67 illustrations. 294pp. 5⅜ x 8½. 20326-3 Pa. $5.95

ANARCHISM AND OTHER ESSAYS, Emma Goldman. Powerful, penetrating, prophetic essays on direct action, role of minorities, prison reform, puritan hypocrisy, violence, etc. 271pp. 5⅜ x 8½. 22484-8 Pa. $6.95

MYTHS OF THE HINDUS AND BUDDHISTS, Ananda K. Coomaraswamy and Sister Nivedita. Great stories of the epics; deeds of Krishna, Shiva, taken from puranas, Vedas, folk tales; etc. 32 illustrations. 400pp. 5⅜ x 8½. 21759-0 Pa. $10.95

BEYOND PSYCHOLOGY, Otto Rank. Fear of death, desire of immortality, nature of sexuality, social organization, creativity, according to Rankian system. 291pp. 5⅜ x 8½. 20485-5 Pa. $8.95

A THEOLOGICO-POLITICAL TREATISE, Benedict Spinoza. Also contains unfinished Political Treatise. Great classic on religious liberty, theory of government on common consent. R. Elwes translation. Total of 421pp. 5⅜ x 8½. 20249-6 Pa. $9.95

CATALOG OF DOVER BOOKS

MY BONDAGE AND MY FREEDOM, Frederick Douglass. Born a slave, Douglass became outspoken force in antislavery movement. The best of Douglass' autobiographies. Graphic description of slave life. 464pp. 5⅜ x 8½. 22457-0 Pa. $8.95

FOLLOWING THE EQUATOR: A Journey Around the World, Mark Twain. Fascinating humorous account of 1897 voyage to Hawaii, Australia, India, New Zealand, etc. Ironic, bemused reports on peoples, customs, climate, flora and fauna, politics, much more. 197 illustrations. 720pp. 5⅜ x 8½. 26113-1 Pa. $15.95

THE PEOPLE CALLED SHAKERS, Edward D. Andrews. Definitive study of Shakers: origins, beliefs, practices, dances, social organization, furniture and crafts, etc. 33 illustrations. 351pp. 5⅜ x 8½. 21081-2 Pa. $8.95

THE MYTHS OF GREECE AND ROME, H. A. Guerber. A classic of mythology, generously illustrated, long prized for its simple, graphic, accurate retelling of the principal myths of Greece and Rome, and for its commentary on their origins and significance. With 64 illustrations by Michelangelo, Raphael, Titian, Rubens, Canova, Bernini and others. 480pp. 5⅜ x 8½. 27584-1 Pa. $9.95

PSYCHOLOGY OF MUSIC, Carl E. Seashore. Classic work discusses music as a medium from psychological viewpoint. Clear treatment of physical acoustics, auditory apparatus, sound perception, development of musical skills, nature of musical feeling, host of other topics. 88 figures. 408pp. 5⅜ x 8½. 21851-1 Pa. $10.95

THE PHILOSOPHY OF HISTORY, Georg W. Hegel. Great classic of Western thought develops concept that history is not chance but rational process, the evolution of freedom. 457pp. 5⅜ x 8½. 20112-0 Pa. $9.95

THE BOOK OF TEA, Kakuzo Okakura. Minor classic of the Orient: entertaining, charming explanation, interpretation of traditional Japanese culture in terms of tea ceremony. 94pp. 5⅜ x 8½. 20070-1 Pa. $3.95

LIFE IN ANCIENT EGYPT, Adolf Erman. Fullest, most thorough, detailed older account with much not in more recent books, domestic life, religion, magic, medicine, commerce, much more. Many illustrations reproduce tomb paintings, carvings, hieroglyphs, etc. 597pp. 5⅜ x 8½. 22632-8 Pa. $11.95

SUNDIALS, Their Theory and Construction, Albert Waugh. Far and away the best, most thorough coverage of ideas, mathematics concerned, types, construction, adjusting anywhere. Simple, nontechnical treatment allows even children to build several of these dials. Over 100 illustrations. 230pp. 5⅜ x 8½. 22947-5 Pa. $7.95

DYNAMICS OF FLUIDS IN POROUS MEDIA, Jacob Bear. For advanced students of ground water hydrology, soil mechanics and physics, drainage and irrigation engineering, and more. 335 illustrations. Exercises, with answers. 784pp. 6⅛ x 9¼. 65675-6 Pa. $19.95

SONGS OF EXPERIENCE: Facsimile Reproduction with 26 Plates in Full Color, William Blake. 26 full-color plates from a rare 1826 edition. Includes "TheTyger," "London," "Holy Thursday," and other poems. Printed text of poems. 48pp. 5¼ x 7. 24636-1 Pa. $4.95

OLD-TIME VIGNETTES IN FULL COLOR, Carol Belanger Grafton (ed.). Over 390 charming, often sentimental illustrations, selected from archives of Victorian graphics—pretty women posing, children playing, food, flowers, kittens and puppies, smiling cherubs, birds and butterflies, much more. All copyright-free. 48pp. 9¼ x 12¼. 27269-9 Pa. $5.95

PERSPECTIVE FOR ARTISTS, Rex Vicat Cole. Depth, perspective of sky and sea, shadows, much more, not usually covered. 391 diagrams, 81 reproductions of drawings and paintings. 279pp. 5⅜ x 8½. 22487-2 Pa. $6.95

DRAWING THE LIVING FIGURE, Joseph Sheppard. Innovative approach to artistic anatomy focuses on specifics of surface anatomy, rather than muscles and bones. Over 170 drawings of live models in front, back and side views, and in widely varying poses. Accompanying diagrams. 177 illustrations. Introduction. Index. 144pp. 8⅜ x11¼. 26723-7 Pa. $8.95

GOTHIC AND OLD ENGLISH ALPHABETS: 100 Complete Fonts, Dan X. Solo. Add power, elegance to posters, signs, other graphics with 100 stunning copyright-free alphabets: Blackstone, Dolbey, Germania, 97 more–including many lower-case, numerals, punctuation marks. 104pp. 8⅛ x 11. 24695-7 Pa. $8.95

HOW TO DO BEADWORK, Mary White. Fundamental book on craft from simple projects to five-bead chains and woven works. 106 illustrations. 142pp. 5⅜ x 8. 20697-1 Pa. $4.95

THE BOOK OF WOOD CARVING, Charles Marshall Sayers. Finest book for beginners discusses fundamentals and offers 34 designs. "Absolutely first rate . . . well thought out and well executed."–E. J. Tangerman. 118pp. 7¾ x 10⅝. 23654-4 Pa. $6.95

ILLUSTRATED CATALOG OF CIVIL WAR MILITARY GOODS: Union Army Weapons, Insignia, Uniform Accessories, and Other Equipment, Schuyler, Hartley, and Graham. Rare, profusely illustrated 1846 catalog includes Union Army uniform and dress regulations, arms and ammunition, coats, insignia, flags, swords, rifles, etc. 226 illustrations. 160pp. 9 x 12. 24939-5 Pa. $10.95

WOMEN'S FASHIONS OF THE EARLY 1900s: An Unabridged Republication of "New York Fashions, 1909," National Cloak & Suit Co. Rare catalog of mail-order fashions documents women's and children's clothing styles shortly after the turn of the century. Captions offer full descriptions, prices. Invaluable resource for fashion, costume historians. Approximately 725 illustrations. 128pp. 8⅜ x 11¼. 27276-1 Pa. $11.95

THE 1912 AND 1915 GUSTAV STICKLEY FURNITURE CATALOGS, Gustav Stickley. With over 200 detailed illustrations and descriptions, these two catalogs are essential reading and reference materials and identification guides for Stickley furniture. Captions cite materials, dimensions and prices. 112pp. 6½ x 9¼. 26676-1 Pa. $9.95

EARLY AMERICAN LOCOMOTIVES, John H. White, Jr. Finest locomotive engravings from early 19th century: historical (1804–74), main-line (after 1870), special, foreign, etc. 147 plates. 142pp. 11⅜ x 8¼. 22772-3 Pa. $10.95

THE TALL SHIPS OF TODAY IN PHOTOGRAPHS, Frank O. Braynard. Lavishly illustrated tribute to nearly 100 majestic contemporary sailing vessels: Amerigo Vespucci, Clearwater, Constitution, Eagle, Mayflower, Sea Cloud, Victory, many more. Authoritative captions provide statistics, background on each ship. 190 black-and-white photographs and illustrations. Introduction. 128pp. 8⅞ x 11¾. 27163-3 Pa. $13.95

EARLY NINETEENTH-CENTURY CRAFTS AND TRADES, Peter Stockham (ed.). Extremely rare 1807 volume describes to youngsters the crafts and trades of the day: brickmaker, weaver, dressmaker, bookbinder, ropemaker, saddler, many more. Quaint prose, charming illustrations for each craft. 20 black-and-white line illustrations. 192pp. 4⅝ x 6.   27293-1 Pa. $4.95

VICTORIAN FASHIONS AND COSTUMES FROM HARPER'S BAZAR, 1867–1898, Stella Blum (ed.). Day costumes, evening wear, sports clothes, shoes, hats, other accessories in over 1,000 detailed engravings. 320pp. 9⅜ x 12¼.
22990-4 Pa. $14.95

GUSTAV STICKLEY, THE CRAFTSMAN, Mary Ann Smith. Superb study surveys broad scope of Stickley's achievement, especially in architecture. Design philosophy, rise and fall of the Craftsman empire, descriptions and floor plans for many Craftsman houses, more. 86 black-and-white halftones. 31 line illustrations. Introduction 208pp. 6½ x 9¼.   27210-9 Pa. $9.95

THE LONG ISLAND RAIL ROAD IN EARLY PHOTOGRAPHS, Ron Ziel. Over 220 rare photos, informative text document origin (1844) and development of rail service on Long Island. Vintage views of early trains, locomotives, stations, passengers, crews, much more. Captions. 8⅞ x 11¾.   26301-0 Pa. $13.95

THE BOOK OF OLD SHIPS: From Egyptian Galleys to Clipper Ships, Henry B. Culver. Superb, authoritative history of sailing vessels, with 80 magnificent line illustrations. Galley, bark, caravel, longship, whaler, many more. Detailed, informative text on each vessel by noted naval historian. Introduction. 256pp. 5⅜ x 8½.
27332-6 Pa. $7.95

TEN BOOKS ON ARCHITECTURE, Vitruvius. The most important book ever written on architecture. Early Roman aesthetics, technology, classical orders, site selection, all other aspects. Morgan translation. 331pp. 5⅜ x 8½.   20645-9 Pa. $8.95

THE HUMAN FIGURE IN MOTION, Eadweard Muybridge. More than 4,500 stopped-action photos, in action series, showing undraped men, women, children jumping, lying down, throwing, sitting, wrestling, carrying, etc. 390pp. 7⅞ x 10⅝.
20204-6 Clothbd. $25.95

TREES OF THE EASTERN AND CENTRAL UNITED STATES AND CANADA, William M. Harlow. Best one-volume guide to 140 trees. Full descriptions, woodlore, range, etc. Over 600 illustrations. Handy size. 288pp. 4½ x 6⅜.
20395-6 Pa. $5.95

SONGS OF WESTERN BIRDS, Dr. Donald J. Borror. Complete song and call repertoire of 60 western species, including flycatchers, juncoes, cactus wrens, many more–includes fully illustrated booklet.   Cassette and manual 99913-0 $8.95

GROWING AND USING HERBS AND SPICES, Milo Miloradovich. Versatile handbook provides all the information needed for cultivation and use of all the herbs and spices available in North America. 4 illustrations. Index. Glossary. 236pp. 5⅜ x 8½.
25058-X Pa. $6.95

BIG BOOK OF MAZES AND LABYRINTHS, Walter Shepherd. 50 mazes and labyrinths in all–classical, solid, ripple, and more–in one great volume. Perfect inexpensive puzzler for clever youngsters. Full solutions. 112pp. 8⅛ x 11.
22951-3 Pa. $4.95

CATALOG OF DOVER BOOKS

PIANO TUNING, J. Cree Fischer. Clearest, best book for beginner, amateur. Simple repairs, raising dropped notes, tuning by easy method of flattened fifths. No previous skills needed. 4 illustrations. 201pp. 5⅜ x 8½. 23267-0 Pa. $6.95

A SOURCE BOOK IN THEATRICAL HISTORY, A. M. Nagler. Contemporary observers on acting, directing, make-up, costuming, stage props, machinery, scene design, from Ancient Greece to Chekhov. 611pp. 5⅜ x 8½. 20515-0 Pa. $12.95

THE COMPLETE NONSENSE OF EDWARD LEAR, Edward Lear. All nonsense limericks, zany alphabets, Owl and Pussycat, songs, nonsense botany, etc., illustrated by Lear. Total of 320pp. 5⅜ x 8½. (USO) 20167-8 Pa. $6.95

VICTORIAN PARLOUR POETRY: An Annotated Anthology, Michael R. Turner. 117 gems by Longfellow, Tennyson, Browning, many lesser-known poets. "The Village Blacksmith," "Curfew Must Not Ring Tonight," "Only a Baby Small," dozens more, often difficult to find elsewhere. Index of poets, titles, first lines. xxiii + 325pp. 5⅜ x 8¼. 27044-0 Pa. $8.95

DUBLINERS, James Joyce. Fifteen stories offer vivid, tightly focused observations of the lives of Dublin's poorer classes. At least one, "The Dead," is considered a masterpiece. Reprinted complete and unabridged from standard edition. 160pp. 5³⁄₁₆ x 8¼. 26870-5 Pa. $1.00

THE HAUNTED MONASTERY and THE CHINESE MAZE MURDERS, Robert van Gulik. Two full novels by van Gulik, set in 7th-century China, continue adventures of Judge Dee and his companions. An evil Taoist monastery, seemingly supernatural events; overgrown topiary maze hides strange crimes. 27 illustrations. 328pp. 5⅜ x 8½. 23502-5 Pa. $8.95

THE BOOK OF THE SACRED MAGIC OF ABRAMELIN THE MAGE, translated by S. MacGregor Mathers. Medieval manuscript of ceremonial magic. Basic document in Aleister Crowley, Golden Dawn groups. 268pp. 5⅜ x 8½. 23211-5 Pa. $8.95

NEW RUSSIAN-ENGLISH AND ENGLISH-RUSSIAN DICTIONARY, M. A. O'Brien. This is a remarkably handy Russian dictionary, containing a surprising amount of information, including over 70,000 entries. 366pp. 4½ x 6⅛. 20208-9 Pa. $9.95

HISTORIC HOMES OF THE AMERICAN PRESIDENTS, Second, Revised Edition, Irvin Haas. A traveler's guide to American Presidential homes, most open to the public, depicting and describing homes occupied by every American President from George Washington to George Bush. With visiting hours, admission charges, travel routes. 175 photographs. Index. 160pp. 8¼ x 11. 26751-2 Pa. $11.95

NEW YORK IN THE FORTIES, Andreas Feininger. 162 brilliant photographs by the well-known photographer, formerly with *Life* magazine. Commuters, shoppers, Times Square at night, much else from city at its peak. Captions by John von Hartz. 181pp. 9¼ x 10¾. 23585-8 Pa. $12.95

INDIAN SIGN LANGUAGE, William Tomkins. Over 525 signs developed by Sioux and other tribes. Written instructions and diagrams. Also 290 pictographs. 111pp. 6⅛ x 9¼. 22029-X Pa. $3.95

CATALOG OF DOVER BOOKS

ANATOMY: A Complete Guide for Artists, Joseph Sheppard. A master of figure drawing shows artists how to render human anatomy convincingly. Over 460 illustrations. 224pp. 8⅜ x 11¼. 27279-6 Pa. $10.95

MEDIEVAL CALLIGRAPHY: Its History and Technique, Marc Drogin. Spirited history, comprehensive instruction manual covers 13 styles (ca. 4th century thru 15th). Excellent photographs; directions for duplicating medieval techniques with modern tools. 224pp. 8⅜ x 11¼. 26142-5 Pa. $11.95

DRIED FLOWERS: How to Prepare Them, Sarah Whitlock and Martha Rankin. Complete instructions on how to use silica gel, meal and borax, perlite aggregate, sand and borax, glycerine and water to create attractive permanent flower arrangements. 12 illustrations. 32pp. 5⅜ x 8½. 21802-3 Pa. $1.00

EASY-TO-MAKE BIRD FEEDERS FOR WOODWORKERS, Scott D. Campbell. Detailed, simple-to-use guide for designing, constructing, caring for and using feeders. Text, illustrations for 12 classic and contemporary designs. 96pp. 5⅜ x 8½. 25847-5 Pa. $2.95

SCOTTISH WONDER TALES FROM MYTH AND LEGEND, Donald A. Mackenzie. 16 lively tales tell of giants rumbling down mountainsides, of a magic wand that turns stone pillars into warriors, of gods and goddesses, evil hags, powerful forces and more. 240pp. 5⅜ x 8½. 29677-6 Pa. $6.95

THE HISTORY OF UNDERCLOTHES, C. Willett Cunnington and Phyllis Cunnington. Fascinating, well-documented survey covering six centuries of English undergarments, enhanced with over 100 illustrations: 12th-century laced-up bodice, footed long drawers (1795), 19th-century bustles, 19th-century corsets for men, Victorian "bust improvers," much more. 272pp. 5⅜ x 8¼. 27124-2 Pa. $9.95

ARTS AND CRAFTS FURNITURE: The Complete Brooks Catalog of 1912, Brooks Manufacturing Co. Photos and detailed descriptions of more than 150 now very collectible furniture designs from the Arts and Crafts movement depict davenports, settees, buffets, desks, tables, chairs, bedsteads, dressers and more, all built of solid, quarter-sawed oak. Invaluable for students and enthusiasts of antiques, Americana and the decorative arts. 80pp. 6½ x 9¼. 27471-3 Pa. $7.95

HOW WE INVENTED THE AIRPLANE: An Illustrated History, Orville Wright. Fascinating firsthand account covers early experiments, construction of planes and motors, first flights, much more. Introduction and commentary by Fred C. Kelly. 76 photographs. 96pp. 8¼ x 11. 25662-6 Pa. $8.95

THE ARTS OF THE SAILOR: Knotting, Splicing and Ropework, Hervey Garrett Smith. Indispensable shipboard reference covers tools, basic knots and useful hitches; handsewing and canvas work, more. Over 100 illustrations. Delightful reading for sea lovers. 256pp. 5⅜ x 8½. 26440-8 Pa. $7.95

FRANK LLOYD WRIGHT'S FALLINGWATER: The House and Its History, Second, Revised Edition, Donald Hoffmann. A total revision–both in text and illustrations–of the standard document on Fallingwater, the boldest, most personal architectural statement of Wright's mature years, updated with valuable new material from the recently opened Frank Lloyd Wright Archives. "Fascinating"–*The New York Times*. 116 illustrations. 128pp. 9¼ x 10¾. 27430-6 Pa. $11.95

AUTOBIOGRAPHY: The Story of My Experiments with Truth, Mohandas K. Gandhi. Boyhood, legal studies, purification, the growth of the Satyagraha (nonviolent protest) movement. Critical, inspiring work of the man responsible for the freedom of India. 480pp. 5⅜ x 8½. (USO) 24593-4 Pa. $8.95

CELTIC MYTHS AND LEGENDS, T. W. Rolleston. Masterful retelling of Irish and Welsh stories and tales. Cuchulain, King Arthur, Deirdre, the Grail, many more. First paperback edition. 58 full-page illustrations. 512pp. 5⅜ x 8½. 26507-2 Pa. $9.95

THE PRINCIPLES OF PSYCHOLOGY, William James. Famous long course complete, unabridged. Stream of thought, time perception, memory, experimental methods; great work decades ahead of its time. 94 figures. 1,391pp. 5⅜ x 8½. 2-vol. set.
Vol. I: 20381-6 Pa. $12.95
Vol. II: 20382-4 Pa. $12.95

THE WORLD AS WILL AND REPRESENTATION, Arthur Schopenhauer. Definitive English translation of Schopenhauer's life work, correcting more than 1,000 errors, omissions in earlier translations. Translated by E. F. J. Payne. Total of 1,269pp. 5⅜ x 8½. 2-vol. set.
Vol. 1: 21761-2 Pa. $11.95
Vol. 2: 21762-0 Pa. $11.95

MAGIC AND MYSTERY IN TIBET, Madame Alexandra David-Neel. Experiences among lamas, magicians, sages, sorcerers, Bonpa wizards. A true psychic discovery. 32 illustrations. 321pp. 5⅜ x 8½. (USO) 22682-4 Pa. $8.95

THE EGYPTIAN BOOK OF THE DEAD, E. A. Wallis Budge. Complete reproduction of Ani's papyrus, finest ever found. Full hieroglyphic text, interlinear transliteration, word-for-word translation, smooth translation. 533pp. 6½ x 9¼.
21866-X Pa. $10.95

MATHEMATICS FOR THE NONMATHEMATICIAN, Morris Kline. Detailed, college-level treatment of mathematics in cultural and historical context, with numerous exercises. Recommended Reading Lists. Tables. Numerous figures. 641pp. 5⅜ x 8½.
24823-2 Pa. $11.95

THEORY OF WING SECTIONS: Including a Summary of Airfoil Data, Ira H. Abbott and A. E. von Doenhoff. Concise compilation of subsonic aerodynamic characteristics of NACA wing sections, plus description of theory. 350pp. of tables. 693pp. 5⅜ x 8½. 60586-8 Pa. $14.95

THE RIME OF THE ANCIENT MARINER, Gustave Doré, S. T. Coleridge. Doré's finest work; 34 plates capture moods, subtleties of poem. Flawless full-size reproductions printed on facing pages with authoritative text of poem. "Beautiful. Simply beautiful."–*Publisher's Weekly.* 77pp. 9¼ x 12. 22305-1 Pa. $6.95

NORTH AMERICAN INDIAN DESIGNS FOR ARTISTS AND CRAFTSPEOPLE, Eva Wilson. Over 360 authentic copyright-free designs adapted from Navajo blankets, Hopi pottery, Sioux buffalo hides, more. Geometrics, symbolic figures, plant and animal motifs, etc. 128pp. 8⅜ x 11. (EUK) 25341-4 Pa. $8.95

SCULPTURE: Principles and Practice, Louis Slobodkin. Step-by-step approach to clay, plaster, metals, stone; classical and modern. 253 drawings, photos. 255pp. 8⅛ x 11.
22960-2 Pa. $10.95

PHOTOGRAPHIC SKETCHBOOK OF THE CIVIL WAR, Alexander Gardner. 100 photos taken on field during the Civil War. Famous shots of Manassas Harper's Ferry, Lincoln, Richmond, slave pens, etc. 244pp. 10⅝ x 8¼.   22731-6 Pa. $9.95

FIVE ACRES AND INDEPENDENCE, Maurice G. Kains. Great back-to-the-land classic explains basics of self-sufficient farming. The one book to get. 95 illustrations. 397pp. 5⅜ x 8½.   20974-1 Pa. $7.95

SONGS OF EASTERN BIRDS, Dr. Donald J. Borror. Songs and calls of 60 species most common to eastern U.S.: warblers, woodpeckers, flycatchers, thrushes, larks, many more in high-quality recording.   Cassette and manual 99912-2 $8.95

A MODERN HERBAL, Margaret Grieve. Much the fullest, most exact, most useful compilation of herbal material. Gigantic alphabetical encyclopedia, from aconite to zedoary, gives botanical information, medical properties, folklore, economic uses, much else. Indispensable to serious reader. 161 illustrations. 888pp. 6½ x 9¼. 2-vol. set. (USO)   Vol. I: 22798-7 Pa. $9.95
Vol. II: 22799-5 Pa. $9.95

HIDDEN TREASURE MAZE BOOK, Dave Phillips. Solve 34 challenging mazes accompanied by heroic tales of adventure. Evil dragons, people-eating plants, blood-thirsty giants, many more dangerous adversaries lurk at every twist and turn. 34 mazes, stories, solutions. 48pp. 8¼ x 11.   24566-7 Pa. $2.95

LETTERS OF W. A. MOZART, Wolfgang A. Mozart. Remarkable letters show bawdy wit, humor, imagination, musical insights, contemporary musical world; includes some letters from Leopold Mozart. 276pp. 5⅜ x 8½.   22859-2 Pa. $7.95

BASIC PRINCIPLES OF CLASSICAL BALLET, Agrippina Vaganova. Great Russian theoretician, teacher explains methods for teaching classical ballet. 118 illus-trations. 175pp. 5⅜ x 8½.   22036-2 Pa. $5.95

THE JUMPING FROG, Mark Twain. Revenge edition. The original story of The Celebrated Jumping Frog of Calaveras County, a hapless French translation, and Twain's hilarious "retranslation" from the French. 12 illustrations. 66pp. 5⅜ x 8½.
22686-7 Pa. $3.95

BEST REMEMBERED POEMS, Martin Gardner (ed.). The 126 poems in this superb collection of 19th- and 20th-century British and American verse range from Shelley's "To a Skylark" to the impassioned "Renascence" of Edna St. Vincent Millay and to Edward Lear's whimsical "The Owl and the Pussycat." 224pp. 5⅜ x 8½.
27165-X Pa. $4.95

COMPLETE SONNETS, William Shakespeare. Over 150 exquisite poems deal with love, friendship, the tyranny of time, beauty's evanescence, death and other themes in language of remarkable power, precision and beauty. Glossary of archaic terms. 80pp. 5³⁄₁₆ x 8¼.   26686-9 Pa. $1.00

BODIES IN A BOOKSHOP, R. T. Campbell. Challenging mystery of blackmail and murder with ingenious plot and superbly drawn characters. In the best tradition of British suspense fiction. 192pp. 5⅜ x 8½.   24720-1 Pa. $6.95

THE WIT AND HUMOR OF OSCAR WILDE, Alvin Redman (ed.). More than 1,000 ripostes, paradoxes, wisecracks: Work is the curse of the drinking classes; I can resist everything except temptation; etc. 258pp. 5⅜ x 8½.   20602-5 Pa. $5.95

SHAKESPEARE LEXICON AND QUOTATION DICTIONARY, Alexander Schmidt. Full definitions, locations, shades of meaning in every word in plays and poems. More than 50,000 exact quotations. 1,485pp. 6½ x 9¼. 2-vol. set.
Vol. 1: 22726-X Pa. $16.95
Vol. 2: 22727-8 Pa. $16.95

SELECTED POEMS, Emily Dickinson. Over 100 best-known, best-loved poems by one of America's foremost poets, reprinted from authoritative early editions. No comparable edition at this price. Index of first lines. 64pp. 5³⁄₁₆ x 8¼.
26466-1 Pa. $1.00

CELEBRATED CASES OF JUDGE DEE (DEE GOONG AN), translated by Robert van Gulik. Authentic 18th-century Chinese detective novel; Dee and associates solve three interlocked cases. Led to van Gulik's own stories with same characters. Extensive introduction. 9 illustrations. 237pp. 5⅜ x 8½.   23337-5 Pa. $6.95

THE MALLEUS MALEFICARUM OF KRAMER AND SPRENGER, translated by Montague Summers. Full text of most important witchhunter's "bible," used by both Catholics and Protestants. 278pp. 6⅝ x 10.   22802-9 Pa. $12.95

SPANISH STORIES/CUENTOS ESPAÑOLES: A Dual-Language Book, Angel Flores (ed.). Unique format offers 13 great stories in Spanish by Cervantes, Borges, others. Faithful English translations on facing pages. 352pp. 5⅜ x 8½.
25399-6 Pa. $8.95

THE CHICAGO WORLD'S FAIR OF 1893: A Photographic Record, Stanley Appelbaum (ed.). 128 rare photos show 200 buildings, Beaux-Arts architecture, Midway, original Ferris Wheel, Edison's kinetoscope, more. Architectural emphasis; full text. 116pp. 8¼ x 11.   23990-X Pa. $9.95

OLD QUEENS, N.Y., IN EARLY PHOTOGRAPHS, Vincent F. Seyfried and William Asadorian. Over 160 rare photographs of Maspeth, Jamaica, Jackson Heights, and other areas. Vintage views of DeWitt Clinton mansion, 1939 World's Fair and more. Captions. 192pp. 8⅞ x 11.   26358-4 Pa. $12.95

CAPTURED BY THE INDIANS: 15 Firsthand Accounts, 1750-1870, Frederick Drimmer. Astounding true historical accounts of grisly torture, bloody conflicts, relentless pursuits, miraculous escapes and more, by people who lived to tell the tale. 384pp. 5⅜ x 8½.   24901-8 Pa. $8.95

THE WORLD'S GREAT SPEECHES, Lewis Copeland and Lawrence W. Lamm (eds.). Vast collection of 278 speeches of Greeks to 1970. Powerful and effective models; unique look at history. 842pp. 5⅜ x 8½.   20468-5 Pa. $14.95

THE BOOK OF THE SWORD, Sir Richard F. Burton. Great Victorian scholar/adventurer's eloquent, erudite history of the "queen of weapons"–from prehistory to early Roman Empire. Evolution and development of early swords, variations (sabre, broadsword, cutlass, scimitar, etc.), much more. 336pp. 6⅛ x 9¼.
25434-8 Pa. $9.95

THE INFLUENCE OF SEA POWER UPON HISTORY, 1660–1783, A. T. Mahan. Influential classic of naval history and tactics still used as text in war colleges. First paperback edition. 4 maps. 24 battle plans. 640pp. 5⅜ x 8½. 25509-3 Pa. $12.95

THE STORY OF THE TITANIC AS TOLD BY ITS SURVIVORS, Jack Winocour (ed.). What it was really like. Panic, despair, shocking inefficiency, and a little heroism. More thrilling than any fictional account. 26 illustrations. 320pp. 5⅜ x 8½. 20610-6 Pa. $8.95

FAIRY AND FOLK TALES OF THE IRISH PEASANTRY, William Butler Yeats (ed.). Treasury of 64 tales from the twilight world of Celtic myth and legend: "The Soul Cages," "The Kildare Pooka," "King O'Toole and his Goose," many more. Introduction and Notes by W. B. Yeats. 352pp. 5⅜ x 8½. 26941-8 Pa. $8.95

BUDDHIST MAHAYANA TEXTS, E. B. Cowell and Others (eds.). Superb, accurate translations of basic documents in Mahayana Buddhism, highly important in history of religions. The Buddha-karita of Asvaghosha, Larger Sukhavativyuha, more. 448pp. 5⅜ x 8½. 25552-2 Pa. $9.95

ONE TWO THREE . . . INFINITY: Facts and Speculations of Science, George Gamow. Great physicist's fascinating, readable overview of contemporary science: number theory, relativity, fourth dimension, entropy, genes, atomic structure, much more. 128 illustrations. Index. 352pp. 5⅜ x 8½. 25664-2 Pa. $8.95

ENGINEERING IN HISTORY, Richard Shelton Kirby, et al. Broad, nontechnical survey of history's major technological advances: birth of Greek science, industrial revolution, electricity and applied science, 20th-century automation, much more. 181 illustrations. ". . . excellent . . ."–*Isis.* Bibliography. vii + 530pp. 5⅜ x 8¼. 26412-2 Pa. $14.95

DALÍ ON MODERN ART: The Cuckolds of Antiquated Modern Art, Salvador Dalí. Influential painter skewers modern art and its practitioners. Outrageous evaluations of Picasso, Cézanne, Turner, more. 15 renderings of paintings discussed. 44 calligraphic decorations by Dalí. 96pp. 5⅜ x 8½. (USO) 29220-7 Pa. $4.95

ANTIQUE PLAYING CARDS: A Pictorial History, Henry René D'Allemagne. Over 900 elaborate, decorative images from rare playing cards (14th–20th centuries): Bacchus, death, dancing dogs, hunting scenes, royal coats of arms, players cheating, much more. 96pp. 9¼ x 12¼. 29265-7 Pa. $11.95

MAKING FURNITURE MASTERPIECES: 30 Projects with Measured Drawings, Franklin H. Gottshall. Step-by-step instructions, illustrations for constructing handsome, useful pieces, among them a Sheraton desk, Chippendale chair, Spanish desk, Queen Anne table and a William and Mary dressing mirror. 224pp. 8⅛ x 11¼. 29338-6 Pa. $13.95

THE FOSSIL BOOK: A Record of Prehistoric Life, Patricia V. Rich et al. Profusely illustrated definitive guide covers everything from single-celled organisms and dinosaurs to birds and mammals and the interplay between climate and man. Over 1,500 illustrations. 760pp. 7½ x 10⅛. 29371-8 Pa. $29.95

Prices subject to change without notice.

Available at your book dealer or write for free catalog to Dept. GI, Dover Publications, Inc., 31 East 2nd St., Mineola, N.Y. 11501. Dover publishes more than 500 books each year on science, elementary and advanced mathematics, biology, music, art, literary history, social sciences and other areas.